Uses of Literature

Tatiana Tilly

Uses of Literature

The Social Dimensions of Literature

University Press of Southern Denmark 2022

© The author and University Press of Southern Denmark 2022
University of Southern Denmark Studies in Scandinavian Languages
and Literatures vol. 149
Printed by Narayana Press
Cover by Dorthe Møller, Unisats Aps
Photos by: David Binzer
ISBN 978-87-408-3410-9

Uses of Literature is published with support from:
The Danish National Research Foundation (Grant Number DNRF127)

University Press of Southern Denmark
55 Campusvej
DK-5230 Odense M
www.universitypress.dk

Distribution in the United States and Canada:
Independent Publishers Group
www.ipgbook.com

Distribution in the United Kingdom:
Gazelle Books
www.gazellebookservices.co.uk

Content

Opening Remarks 7

Uses of Literature 9

New Sociologies of Literature 15

Gender, Love and Recognition 23

Interdisciplinary research 34

New approaches to teaching 41

Class, Precarity and the Social Dimensions of Literature 45

Narrative Medicine and Medical Humanities 73

The Ten Most Important Publications from 2016-2021 100

Opening Remarks

This report highlights the most important insights, discussions and results that have emerged during the period from 2016 to 2021, in which the Uses of Literature research project has taken place.

The aim has been to document the specific outcomes such as the numerous articles, events and publications that have been realized as a result of the project, but also to share the discussions and reflections that have arisen within the group of researchers, as it is quite unique for the humanities to gather more than twenty researchers from various backgrounds over the course of five years to develop ideas and research in often close collaboration.

Thus, it is the hope that this publication can stimulate further debate and research ideas by sharing the thoughts and knowledge that have been developed as part of the generous and ambitious research environment of Uses of Literature.

This publication was initiated by the managing group of researchers behind the Uses of Literature project at the University of Southern Denmark and is a result of the cooperation between the researchers and the journalist Tatiana Tilly with support from The Danish National Research Foundation (Grant number DNRF127).

Rita Felski
Anne-Marie Mai
Peter Simonsen
Klaus Petersen

Uses of Literature
The Social Dimensions of Literature

Over a period of five years, the project Uses of Literature – The Social Dimensions of Literature (UoL) has worked in ways that are rather extraordinary for scholars of the humanities. A group of more than twenty researchers have collaborated closely, held weekly meetings, co-authored articles, and organized numerous conferences, online seminars and workshops.

Based at the University of Southern Denmark (SDU), Uses of Literature was established in 2016 under the leadership of Anne-Marie Mai, Professor of Danish literature. The project was funded by the Danish National Research Foundation as part of the Niels Bohr professorship, a role that was given to Rita Felski, Professor of English at the University of Virginia and a renowned scholar and expert on literary method, interpretation, and aesthetics. With the professorship followed a grant of 28 million Danish kroner over five years, which made it possible to appoint three professors, two postdocs and four PhD students, and facilitate a great number of events and retreats. The grant created a space for developing new approaches and methods for exploring the social uses of literature and conducting innovative research.

Uses of Literature draws on both the humanities and social sciences, aims to explore the possibilities and uses of literature, and "seeks to offer richer accounts of what literature does and why it matters."

At the very beginning of the collective research project, the group formulated ten theses as a foundation for the further work. The first thesis describes how the essential word *use*, one that can easily trigger controversy among literary scholars, should be understood:

"There are many uses of literature. Use should not be confused with purely instrumental or utilitarian relations to literary works. Perhaps we should speak of the 'usability' of a work rather than its usefulness, to underscore the difference. By 'usability' we mean its capacity to engage readers' concerns and commitments, to inspire recognition, hope, or desire – in both predictable and surprising ways."

Literature is "usable rather than useful in any narrow sense. Its effects are varied, diffuse, unpredictable, indirect, and often long-term; they involve emotion and pleasure as much as ethics or knowledge," as the members of the group describe their mission.

The researchers have worked on various topics through different approaches, methods and theories, but overall they have tried to answer questions such as: "How do we capture the distinctiveness and dynamism of literary works as they move through the world? How can we do justice to the diverse and often surprising ways in which people engage with texts and the many facets of aesthetic experiences? In what ways do literary works speak to matters of concern, inspire attachments, weave affiliations, or forge collectives?"

Anne-Marie Mai, the primary founder of the Uses of Literature project, underlines how important such a big grant is in order to establish an ambitious research group and attract talented international researchers, which among other things has led to an increased number of international publications.

While 2021 was the final year of the project, SDU has established a permanent center for Uses of Literature in order to integrate its achievements into the university and build upon the work that has already been done. This means that Rita Felski and several of the other scholars that were hired as part of the project will be able to continue their engagements at the university in Odense.

This publication describes a selection of the articles that have been written, events that have taken place, as well as discussions that have arisen during the Uses of Literature project; it covers research on new sociologies of literature, actor-network-theory, attachment, recognition, narrative medicine, class, precarity and the social dimensions of literature.

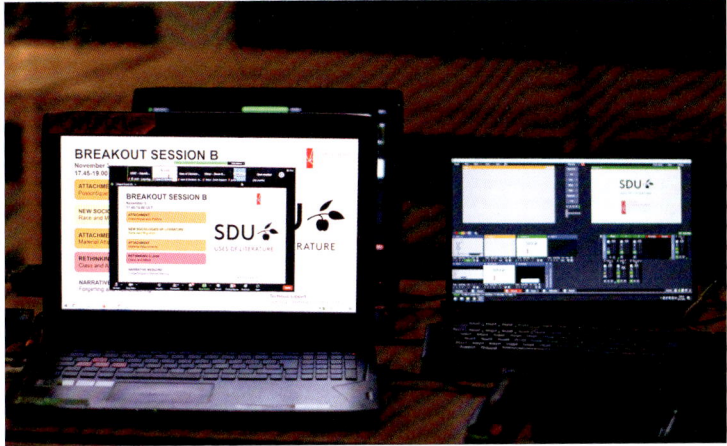

Online setup from the Uses of Literature Final Conference in November 2021
Photo: David Binzer

A wild proposal for Rita Felski

At the beginning of November 2021, a final Uses of Literature conference was held online over three days. Around 300 people had signed up to participate, among them 87 speakers from 19 countries who were interested in discussing some of the topics that have been central for the project.

In her opening speech Rita Felski shared some details about the very beginning of her professorship in Odense:

"Things began, like many adventures do nowadays, with an email. I woke up on March 17, 2015, picked up my phone and saw a message from an unfamiliar name. 'We write out of the blue,' wrote Peter Simonsen, 'with a pretty wild but completely sincere proposal: would you be interested in applying for a five-year Niels Bohr Professorship at the University of Southern Denmark?'" Felski told the online audience.

"The idea was immediately appealing. My daughter had just left for college; I had long dreamed of spending more time in Europe, and I was especially eager to try out other ways of doing research," she said. "To explore alternatives to the solitary and individualist enterprise of locking oneself in a room to work on an

Rita Felski. Photo: David Binzer

article or a book. Within a couple of hours, I had fired back an enthusiastic response."

Her colleague Peter Simonsen remembers this email exchange very clearly, too. Prior to sending it, he had been reading Felski's work with great enthusiasm and shared his interest with Anne-Marie Mai and Klaus Petersen. Over the course of several months, the four professors worked intensively on drafting and rewriting the proposal for the Niels Bohr professorship. They received the good news about a year later. Among the seven awarded professorships, their project was the only one from the humanities and their project was the only of the seven awarded professorships that was granted to the humanities. In her speech, Felski underlined how privileged, important and special it is to be able to work in such a large research group over several years with enough resources to experiment:

"The experience of working as part of a large research group has been eye-opening and life-transforming: conversations unfolding over time, moments of laughter and sometimes passionate debate, a sense of collective commitment and being part of something larger than oneself," Felski said.

"There would be times at SDU – in the midst of an animated discussion – when I would pause for a moment and think to myself how precious it is what I'm experiencing right now: A group of people coming together in a seminar room for two hours, with no other purpose in mind than to hash out their views about a book that interests them."

Hooked: Art and Attachment

During her time at SDU, Felski finished the monograph *Hooked: Art and Attachment,* in which she investigates the dynamics of how and why people become attached to works of art through the perspectives of identification, attunement and interpretation. The book draws on Bruno Latour's actor-network theory (ANT as it is popularly called) to look closely at how people connect to artwork, as she was interested in offering better descriptions of the various forms of attachment we experience.

"We have many philosophical and political accounts of aesthetic experience, but I felt they did not adequately describe what it means to recognize yourself in a book, be struck by a piece of music or cry in front of a painting. I just wanted to slow down the theorizing and look more closely at examples of how people actually engage with books and art and music. So for *Hooked*, I found Latour really useful, because that is what he says: let us not rush to explain, let us try to put aside our prejudices and look very closely at what the relevant actors are doing," Felski explains.

An aspect of Latour's approach that Felski finds helpful, is that it thinks about the chains or links that connect different actors, rather than setting up oppositions: art or society, human or non-human, materialism or idealism. These ideas have been a source of inspiration for several of the scholars in the Uses of Literature project.

Remix: On Literature and Theory

In February and March 2021, Felski gave a series of four Clark Lectures at Cambridge University. As the lectures are very prestigious and required months of preparation, eventually the material turned into a book manuscript called *Remix: Literature, Theory, Life.*

"The book is more philosophically oriented than *Hooked*, but remains deeply interested in the relations between literature and everyday life and has been strongly influenced by the concerns of the Uses of Literature project, especially the working groups on "New Sociologies of Literature" and "Rethinking Class," Felski says.

While some academics have one school of thought they follow during most of their career, Felski sees herself as a pragmatist who tries to answer different questions at different times and seeks for the right theoretical tools for specific problems, with an openness towards new ideas. In her current research, she looks toward the most recent work of German sociologists and philosophers associated with the Frankfurt School in order to address the question of why there is such a lack of connection between literature and the social sciences.

Part of the book deals with the idea of resonance, a concept recently developed by the German social theorist Hartmut Rosa, who describes resonance as being a mode where you come alive through an engagement with something. While people can reach a feeling of resonance through different activities, such as gardening or playing chess, Felski is mainly occupied with resonance through reading or engaging with art.

"Resonance is a powerful way of thinking about our engagement with the words of the dead – or with the words of those who are still alive. We gain a sense of connection to a larger community, to all the people who existed before us and had important and innovative thoughts. Resonance helps explain how engagement with their ideas can be not only intellectually important, but animating, exhilarating, transforming."

The picture is taken at the workshop "ANT Across the Disciplines", September 2017. Photo: David Binzer

New Sociologies of Literature

As a basis of their research, the scholars in Odense have discussed how to reconsider the possibilities and affordances of literature as well as the relations and networks that literary works are parts of. In their ten theses, they describe how literary works can be seen as active participants in these relations. And rather than focusing on what literature *is*, they focus on what literature *does*.

"How do they inspire, mobilize, inform, entertain, captivate, or console readers? How, alternatively, do they shock or provoke?" they write in their second thesis.

Furthermore, they seek to create new sociologies of literature on the basis of Felski's work.

"The aim is to develop new interdisciplinary methods for analyzing the social uses of literature that avoid the reductive tendencies of traditional sociologies of literature. Actor-network theory, especially, offers a fruitful resource for investigating aesthetic attachments and offering richer and more nuanced accounts of how literature circulates in the world. Researchers engaged in distinct yet related projects will take their orientation from Rita Felski's work, especially *Uses of Literature*, *The Limits of Critique*, and her current book on attachment, and her *NLH* volume on "New Sociologies of Literature," to develop innovative forms of interaction between literature and the social sciences."

By using methods and theories that are usually applied in the social sciences, while also revising them, the scholars at SDU attempt in various ways to trace the networks literary works are part of and how they affect the people they are in touch with.

Over the years, Uses of Literature have been visited by scholars such as James English (professor at University of Pennsylvania), Caroline Levine (professor at Cornell University) and Heather Love (professor at University of Pennsylvania) who have given talks on the sociology of literature.

New Approaches to Bob Dylan

The work of Bob Dylan is so dense with literary references and so popular around the world, that Anne-Marie Mai finds it both obvious and valuable to look at his lyrics as networks. Dylan has been a source of inspiration for Mai for years, not only as a musician but also as a poet, which has eventually become a subject of study for the professor, who published the book *Digteren Dylan* in Danish in 2018. The book was published in English under the title *Bob Dylan the poet* the same year and is currently being translated into German.

Something special happened on October 13, 2016. Rita Felski and the Uses of Literature group had their very first meeting, and when it was over, Mai's phone started ringing and continued to do so for days afterwards. Bob Dylan had been awarded the Nobel prize in literature, and Mai spent the following weeks telling journalists and fans about the literary qualities of Dylan's lyrics. This meant that the Dylan research became an integrated part of Uses of Literature, especially for Mai, but for some of her colleagues as well.

In 2018, they organized the two-day conference *New Approaches to Bob Dylan*, which discussed lyrics, performances, personal history, and mass movements concerning Dylan through a meeting

Tobias Skiveren, Anne-Marie Mai, Peter Simonsen and others in conversation at Rita Felski's inaugural lecture, 5. October 2016. Photo: David Binzer.

between different disciplines. The conference was attended by experts from France, Norway, Finland, Ireland, the UK, the US and Denmark.

Mai was elected as board member of The Bob Dylan Archive at Tulsa University in 2018, and in 2021, the online conference Dylan@80 was organized in collaboration between Tulsa University and Uses of Literature.

"We have been working on studying literary texts as actors within networks of several other actors, and it is very meaningful to examine Dylan's lyrics in that perspective," Mai says.

"His texts are able to travel across time, they connect in different ways to other texts, and his lyrics are like mosaics of literary actors working together; from Shakespeare to Scottish or American folk music to Japanese novels. They act in relation to each other and become incredibly exciting textual networks."

The growing field of literary prizes

Lars Handesten, who is Associate Professor of Literature and has participated part-time in Uses of Literature, was frustrated with the limitations of Bourdieu's theoretical frameworks, when he entered the group. The introduction to Latour's actor-network theory came at a fortunate time, as Handesten was struggling with finding the right theoretical framework for his new book *Litteraturen rundt: Aktører i det litterære felt (A tour around Literature: Actors in the Literary Field),* which was published in 2018. Through fruitful discussions with his colleagues in the group, he ended up applying both Bourdieu and Latour, a combination that might not appear compatible but turned out to be incredibly useful for the book.

"Latour's sociological approach allows for a much more dynamic understanding of each actor's motivations and commitments, rather than solely applying Bourdieu's ideas that focus on power structures. Not everything in this world revolves around power and the urge to position yourself in opposition to others. There are many other motivations, passions and personal relations behind actions and developments," Handesten says.

Combining Bourdieu with Latour offered a richer perspective of the many different actors that are involved in creating a literary institution and the dynamics within the literary area that consists of interactions between authors, editors, teachers, critics, librarians and readers.

In his book chapter *Use of Literature,* published in the anthology by the same name (Litteratur i brug, edited by Anne-Marie Mai), Handesten investigates the many different forms of use; authors drawing on other authors or using their books for aesthetic or political purposes, readers using literature as a form of entertainment or social recognition, teachers who have pedagogical aims or politicians or priests using literature as a source of examples of human actions and or societal tendencies.

In his article, *Litterære priser i Danmark (Literary Awards in Denmark),* which has been published by *SPRING,* Handesten conducts a mapping of the literary awards and prizes given in Denmark from 1990 until 2020. As this landscape is constantly changing, with new prizes being introduced and old ones disappearing, Handesten does not claim to give the final picture, but his research contributes with new knowledge and a more precise overview of the field; who gives prizes, who receives them, how many are there and what questions would be interesting to investigate in further research?

Currently, there are more than 50 different literary prizes in Denmark and the number seems to be growing each year. Meanwhile, numerous smaller prizes have been introduced among genres such as horror, fantasy and science fiction, that have their own subcultures in the literary landscape.

This relatively large number triggered Handesten's curiosity, as he was surprised by the amount in such a small language area such as Danish. Besides the mapping, Handesten is interested in understanding the interests that are involved. As an example, many of the larger newspapers have their own literary prizes that create stories for the media to report about, as well as attachment between the papers and their readers, as they often engage them in voting for and celebrating the winner. Thus, it is not only the winning writers who benefit from the existence of a prize, the media themselves gain new editorial content as well as higher reader engagement. In relation to this topic, Handesten drew upon the theories of Rita Felski about the importance of attachment for the readers.

The role of entertainment

The enjoyment of reading is a topic that has been wrongly ignored by literary scholars, according to Handesten. He believes that one of the most obvious motivations for reading is simply entertainment, and that it deserve to be taken more seriously as a topic of research.

In an article, which will be published in the literary journal *Passage,* he draws upon similar research on the topic conducted within media science and cultural studies, since both disciplines have much stronger traditions for investigating the topic.

"The whole point is that entertainment exists as a relation between the reader and the work of art, and people's taste in literature is so diverse that anything can be considered entertaining by someone: some people will find *Ulysses* by James Joyce very amusing, while others would not manage to read a single page without falling asleep. Literary classics can be entertaining too, so it is not just a question of looking at a particular genre of 'entertainment literature' – it is much more complex than that," Handesten says.

Basilisk as a literary actor

Another researcher who has explored examples of the literary institution through the lens of Latour, is Johanne Gormsen Schmidt, who has been in a postdoc position at the University of Copenhagen since September 2020. Although Schmidt is very theoretically oriented, she is equally concerned with how her research can be useful outside academia and in relation to the reading world. When she began her PhD at SDU in 2017, it felt like her perspective and possibilities as a researcher were suddenly widened because of the discussions with Rita Felski and the other members of the Uses of Literature group, and she thus began working in the field of sociology of literature.

"I am especially interested in the question of how to pay attention to real readers' experiences without backing down on one's analytical expertise as a literary scholar. If we want to understand what literature means to people – how it engages us – I think it makes sense to ask people and collect different kinds of readers' stories". Schmidt says. "If you go out and explore empirically what sorts of conversations are going on about literature, where they are taking place, what people are reading, how they are talking about it, then you get the feeling that literature is alive and living well in society", Schmidt says.

Her dissertation, entitled *The Art of Insignificance. Aesthetics and Practice at the Publishing House Basilisk,* seeks to combine literary analysis and sociology by using the small Danish publishing house Basilisk as a case, and investigating the position of Basilisk in Danish literature since 2000.

Schmidt combines qualitative interviews with five of Basilisk's editors and 15 members of their book club, with close readings of selected published works and analyses of the publishing house's

A Uses of Literature seminar in Svendborg, May 2019. Photo: David Binzer

relations to other literary actors as well as their readers. Since Basilisk is still working and developing, the dissertation is a study of a moving, ever changing actor, and Schmidt found it useful to apply and discuss Latour's theories and methodologies as well as Rita Felski's thinking.

"In the process of formulating my approach and daring to do something a bit different, the interdisciplinary activities at the Center – and conversations with Rita Felski – have been invaluable," Schmidt says.

How Covid-19 changed reading habits

There is a direct path from Schmidt's PhD project to the postdoc project she is now working on at the University of Copenhagen, where she is part of a research group called *Lockdown Reading*, which has signed a contract with Oxford University Press for a monograph on the topic. In the project, the group examines how readers have used literature during the Covid-19 pandemic lockdowns in Denmark and the UK.

The drastic changes in everyone's lives during 2020 meant that people who generally identify as readers reported that they had been reading even more than usual, even if they felt under pressure and emotional stress. Schmidt and her colleagues are now analyzing why reading has played such an important role and how the current societal situation affects the experience of reading.

The research on lockdown reading has attracted a lot of attention from outside the academic world, not least from libraries that are interested in understanding the developments of reading habits during the pandemic and seek to adjust their services to the readers' needs. This has meant that Schmidt has been in frequent dialogue with librarians and journalists in addition to the communication she has had with the readers that were the subjects of her case study.

Gender, Love and Recognition

The term recognition can have at least two meanings that are relevant in this context: Firstly, the word holds the meaning of recognizing parts of yourself in a book. Secondly, it refers to the action of recognizing a person or being recognized by someone else, a sort of acknowledgement of a person or their claims. Both types of recognition are of interest to some of the researchers of the Uses of Literature group, who have discussed and applied the concept in their readings and analyzes of literary fiction, to a great degree inspired by Felski's book *Uses of Literature* from 2008, in which she shed new light on the role of recognition in relation to literature.

"Academics have not taken recognition very seriously, because it has often been considered too simple or narcissistic a concept. But I actually think it is a very fundamental part of how one reads", Felski says. "To recognize oneself in a book is not just saying that the character is like me. The point is rather that through reading a novel, perhaps you recognize yourself in a Jane Austen character,

Marie-Elisabeth Lei Holm and Johanne Gormsen Schmidt at a Uses of Literature seminar in Svendborg, May 2019. Photo: David Binzer

but you also get a new perspective on yourself by seeing how that character negotiates her world and perhaps is unaware of her own self-centeredness or insensitivity, so the book can change the way you think about yourself ".

Recognition redefined

One of the scholars investigating the implications of recognition in literature is Marie-Elisabeth Lei Holm, who defended her PhD dissertation, *Recognition Redefined: Using literary texts to get recognition,* in 2020. The dissertation, which will be published as a book with the American publisher Routledge in 2022, explores different aspects of recognition in six selected works of literature. The works deal with race, illness and gender, and the purpose was to investigate how different authors represent societal issues related to recognition. Holm chose to look at contemporary literature (published between 2001 and 2017) by Ta-Nehisi Coates, Yahya Hassan, Maria Gerhardt, Paul Kalanithi, Maja Lucas and Rachel Cusk.

As three of the authors write in Danish and three in English, Holm makes a comparison between the Anglophone and the Danish context throughout the text and takes the societal contexts as well as the popular debates surrounding the works into consideration in her analysis.

"I have looked into different ways in which literature influence political debates, and how it can infiltrate and push public opinion with regards to topics that stir controversy, like motherhood, serious illness and immigration," Holm says.

One of the questions Holm examines is how these "authors articulate calls for recognition via aesthetic means, and what forms of recognition they call for" as well as how these artistic expressions can contribute to sociological and philosophical studies of recognition. Holm argues that literature can create a better understanding of what individuals and social groups seek recognition for, as well as how these claims are manifested. She found that the protagonists seemed to seek recognition for specific lived experiences – and not merely for their identity as someone belonging to a marginalized group.

"Literary texts, along these lines, bring added nuance and fresh perspectives to theories of recognition presented by sociologists and political thinkers," Holm writes.

Essentially, she is interested in what texts do and how literary texts come to matter. Therefore, she applies an understanding of texts as social actors, "capable of affecting moods, changing attitudes, forging bonds, inflicting antagonism and providing comfort", as she writes in her dissertation. Along these lines, Holm emphasizes the potential of literature to change and shape public conversation and our understanding of the world.

"I chose to write about the relation between recognition and contemporary literature given that theories of social acknowledgment can add a lot to our understanding of literary art. At the same time, my aim was to show that those theories can actually benefit from tending to literary aesthetics. From texts, we learn that recognition – being recognized by others as well as giving recognition – is a material and everyday phenomenon, and not a lofty academic concept," Holm says.

Literature in social work

The role of literature in relation to socially vulnerable groups was also the topic of a study Holm conducted of the Danish organization *Læs for Livet (Read for Your Life)*. In the chapter *"I just want to read about someone who has escaped this shit!" – Use of literature in social work*, which was published in the anthology *Litteratur i brug (Use of Literature)*, in the article, Holm describes her fieldwork in which she has followed the organization at meetings with staff, children and adolescents at out-of-home care institutions, where they organize donations of custom-made libraries.

The organization aims to help socially vulnerable children by introducing them to literature and making it accessible in their daily lives. By conducting the case study, Holm observed how the children sought literature that can help them to understand and articulate their own experiences, and looked for books that provide some sort of recognition of their marginalized position – but also books that pointed towards bigger perspectives in order to find inspiration and fuel hope for another way of life.

In addition to her research into literature, recognition and social work, Holm works on projects related to literary arts and health; specifically, the project *Demens ID (Dementia ID)* on literature and dementia.

Adulthoodphobia and questions of motherhood

Adulthoodphobia is a cultural diagnosis, which Camilla Schwartz defines as a resistance towards adult life and the expectations that follow. Schwartz is an Associate Professor in Danish literature and conducts research on topics such as mental illness, welfare studies, cultural theory, and contemporary Nordic literature. During her participation in the Uses of Literature project, she has focused especially on literature related to gender, love and class – and how these themes are interwoven.

In her 2021 book *Take me to Neverland: Voksenfobi og ungdomsdyrkelse i den skandinaviske samtidslitteratur (Take me to Neverland: Adulthoodphobia and Youth Worship in Contemporary Scandinavian Literature)*, Schwartz explores the concept of adulthoodphobia through readings of literature, film, fashion and various cultural products. The term refers to a lifestyle or state of mind, which involves a resistance towards becoming an adult. Elements of revolt against societal norms can be part of the phenomenon, through an unwillingness towards becoming a productive professional in the neoliberal society, but Schwartz does not consider it to be fully a rebellion.

"To resist entering into adult life can be a form of rebellion, but adulthoodphobia also contains elements of submission to the societal ideals of a youthful life: a high degree of mobility, changing tracks professionally, keeping your possibilities open, and not committing to anything fully," Schwartz says. "To insist on being young – not becoming a woman by starving yourself for instance – contains a duality of both rebellion and submission."

In her article *Escaping the urban middle-class scene of adulthood: Adulthoodphobia and the precariat in the work of Hanne Viemose, Theis Ørntoft and Christina Hagen*, Schwartz explores the shapes of adulthoodphobia in contemporary Danish literature, which she connects to issues such as class identity and a fetishization of the precarious life form:

"In these texts the narrative of leaving the ghetto is reversed, producing a strange kind of Bildungsroman. This kind of narrative, too, deals with social mobility, but down the social ladder," Schwartz writes. "This is not always a self-destructive move; in some novels of disillusion, taking the ladder downwards is an attempt to grow (emotionally) and create solidarity with the precarious other. It may seem paradoxical to claim that a text that fetishizes the other at the same time tries to create solidarity with the other. This fetishization works as a caricature of the urban middle class, a class which fears growing up and which therefore refuses to acknowledge its privileges and responsibilities."

In relation to the topic of adulthoodphobia, Schwartz has studied the many recent works dealing with the experience of becoming a mother and the ambivalent feelings that are often depicted. Many female writers have portrayed motherhood with a focus on the fear of losing their youthful life and identity, and transitioning into the new and more static role of the mother: a grown woman with substantial care work and a changed and often less androgynous body.

Schwartz is now working on a book entitled *From Tomboy to Killjoy: Affects, Temporalities and Materiality in Narratives of Non-Parenting,* in which she explores contemporary literary works depicting women who decide against motherhood – and view them from a historical perspective.

"While a youthful lifestyle is idealized when you are a young adult, it is seen as socially unacceptable if you continue living that way when you reach the age of forty. Women who are above forty who have finally decided against motherhood are often or portrayed as monstrous or demonized in popular culture, film and literature," Schwartz says.

While there are few representations of women opting out of motherhood in Danish literature, there are more in the Anglo-Saxon context, such as Chris Kraus, Sheila Heti and Eileen Myles, and Schwartz is convinced that portrayals of the issue will only increase in the near future.

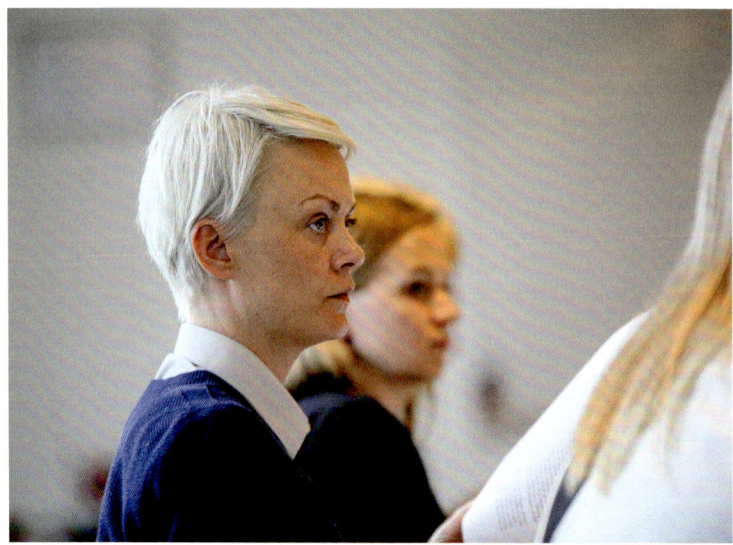

Camilla Schwartz and Marie-Elisabeth Lei Holm at a Uses of Literature seminar in Nyborg, May 2017. Photo: David Binzer

Middle class feminism

Both feminism and class issues are of interest to Schwartz, but as she realized that most works depicting questions concerning feminism were written from a middle class perspective, this group became of special interest to her. In her research, Schwartz applies both class theory and concepts of recognition when she confronts works of art or cultural products. In her analysis of the television documentary *Prinsesser fra Blokken (Princesses from the Block)*, which follows a group of young women living at a concrete housing estate in the outskirts of Copenhagen, Schwartz took her own reactions into consideration as she watched the show, and explored what her own emotional responses can tell her about the perspective of the middle class viewer. It became apparent that she judged the protagonists on the basis of their values, which have traditionally been connected to the working class. Because much of the literature that treat issues related to feminism is written from a middle class perspective, it tends to have a very academic approach that excludes women from the working class or precariat, and thus becomes elitist rather than inclusive, Schwartz argues.

"Something that becomes apparent in some of these texts is the stigmatization of the lower and upper classes, and I am interested in exploring how the middle class is blind to its own classism," she says. "While they are very occupied with fighting racism and climate change, they are unaware of how they exclude people from other parts of society."

Recognition and women's writing

In a collaborative article, Camilla Schwartz and Rita Felski investigate how the idea of recognition can provide new perspectives on contemporary women's writing. By analyzing and comparing the two novels *I Love Dick* by Chris Kraus with *The Other Woman* by Therese Bohman, they focus on what role recognition plays in the two texts – on psychological, as well as political levels.

"The domains of love and esteem seem especially salient to *I Love Dick* and *The Other Woman;* both texts pivot between a pursuit of erotic recognition from a male lover and the desire for validation from female readers," Schwartz and Felski write.

They argue that the two texts "invite rather different experiences of recognition," as the protagonists have different class belongings and different attachments to the ideas and ideals of feminism. Reading and literature play an important role in both novels, however; the protagonists emphasize reading not only as an important activity, but also as part of their identity by orienting themselves in relation to literary characters and seeking recognition for what they read.

"The turn to an imagined reader serves as a way of attaining the recognition that is refused within the diegetic world; recognition from female readers is a salve for the wounds of misrecognition inflicted by the indifference of male lovers. Literature does not just portray a desire for recognition; it *enacts* it," they write.

The meanings of Love, Etc.

Love in contemporary literature, art, and culture was the topic of the conference Love, Etc., which took place at SDU in October 2019 and was organized by Camilla Schwartz, Rita Felski and Anne-Marie Søndergaard Christensen, who is Professor in Practical Philosophy at the Department for the Study of Culture at SDU.

At the conference, a number of international writers and researchers participated to discuss the nature, meanings and challenges of the concept of love and why it is important for the humanities to study the topic at a time when experiences of love seem increasingly fragmented. The two keynote-speakers were Namwali Serpell, who is Professor of English at Harvard University – (and published her first novel in 2019) and the renowned Norwegian author Hanne Ørstavik.

Some of the questions at the center of the discussions at Love, Etc. were: whether love is consistent in its form or changes over time, whether we live in anti-romantic times and how we can speak with nuance and precision about the various meanings and aspects of love. Romantic love, however, was not the only focus at the conference. The scholars were also interested in exploring how love, cognition and knowledge are related – as well as understanding the love of literature, and why readers become attached to certain books. Speakers at the conference also presented their work on topics such as algorithms, dating-apps, politics, ethics and female friendship – all in relation to their perspectives on modern love.

In an interview during the conference, Niels Bohr Professor Rita Felski explained why the scholars found it interesting to organize a conference on love. It is often said that love is everywhere, from Hollywood movies, music and magazines, and love is also the driver of so many aspects of human activity, yet it has largely been neglected in literary studies:

"It has not been completely ignored, but I think there has been a tendency to emphasize perhaps the more negative phenomena in the world. There has been a strong emphasis on conflict, on inequality, and in terms of emotions, there has been a strong emphasis on attitudes such as boredom, anxiety or alienation, rather than happiness or notions of love. And when love has been talked about, there has often been an assumption that it needs to be treated with a certain skepticism or suspicion: Love might be a veil for rather more insidious things going on, so it needs to be questioned or treated as something that is not entirely trustworthy," Felski said.

Given this background, the aims of the conference were to take love seriously in its own terms as a research subject, and to explore alternatives to the word love, synonyms that can better embrace the variety of meanings and objects of love. Felski explained that the ancient Greeks had several different words for love – to express erotic love, love of a friend or love of the divine – whereas we only have one word for love, which means that our contemporary language for love is limited and often dangerously close to becoming a cliché.

Love, Ethics and Literature

At *Love, Etc.*, Professor Anne-Marie Søndergaard Christensen gave a presentation under the title *The Look of Love: Love and Vision*, in which she focused on the connection between love and the act of seeing. Reading recent works by Ali Smith as well as Jennifer Egan's novel *Look at me*, Christensen brought out how being seen can feel equal to being loved and contrasted this with an idea presented by the philosopher Iris Murdoch that attention can be a form of love.

As part of the Uses of Literature group, Christensen has worked on projects on love and attention, love and motherhood and gender identity and transformation, all placed within a wider investigation of the intersection between ethics and literature. Her field of expertise is ethics and in particular contextual ethics, Wittgensteinian ethics, virtue ethics, forms of applied ethics, and the status of moral philosophy. According to Christensen, her participation in the project has led to more collaborations with colleagues at SDU as well as contact to international scholars such as Professor Toril Moi from Duke University, who is a leading literary scholar in the field. (Moi visited SDU in 2017 where she gave a lecture about Knausgård and a seminar about her 2017 book *Revolution of the Ordinary. Literary Studies after Wittgenstein, Austin, and Cavell.*)

Toril Moi at an event in June 2017. Photo: David Binzer

"The emphasis of the uses of literature and attachment have been central for me in the project. More than offering me with new research questions, the project has helped my ongoing work on love, and my investigation of literature as a special field of experience or place of exploring how we are to understand human life," Christensen explains.

What about Swedish romance?
One of the many aspects of love in literature covered in Uses of Literature is the genre of romance novels. Elin Abrahamsson, who is connected to SDU as a visiting postdoc, holds a PhD in gender studies, and wrote a dissertation with the English title *Mas(s)turbatory Readings: A Queer Analysis of Popular Romance* (the original Swedish title is *Enahanda läsning: En queer tolkning av romancegenren)*. Her interest is in feminist cultural studies, queer theory, and "the types of popular culture that are associated with femininity and female audiences, such as boybands and romantic fiction".

On that basis she is now working on a three-year postdoc project, funded by the Swedish Research Council (Vetenskapsrådet), entitled *What About Swedish Romance? Conventions and Communities in Contemporary Swedish Popular Romance*. The project is based at Stockholm University, but implemented mainly at SDU, in affiliation with *Uses of Literature*, and Abrahamsson has been connected to the program since February 2019.

In this current project, she studies "the emergence of and heightened attention to a Swedish popular romance genre; a study which involves both the romantic novels in question and the context in which they are written, read and talked about". In contrast to common perceptions of popular romance, the genre in Sweden is often promoted as feminist. There is a strong focus on gender equality in Swedish romance novels and in the Swedish context more generally. Besides queer theory, the project makes use of theories on post- and popular feminism, as well as critical research on gender equality and exceptionalism. The research group's focus on the social dimensions of literature and on different ways of interacting with cultural texts has been of great relevance to Abrahamsson's work.

"The wide array of seminars, lectures and workshops, offered within the *Uses of Literature* program, has both deepened and widened my thinking on the social dimensions of literature. The range of themes, methods, and perspectives – introduced to me through lectures from invited guests, through the collective reading and discussions of new literary theory, and of course through the readings and discussions of my department colleagues' work – has especially broadened my knowledge and experiences within research fields adjacent to my own."

Interdisciplinary research

Interdisciplinary research is at the heart of the Uses of Literature project, which is manifested in several ways: firstly, through the research that is conducted at SDU, which is highly interdisciplinary due to its collaborative work with scholars as well as theories and methods from fields such as history, anthropology, political science, and health. Secondly, through the research on the use of literature in other disciplines, such as the social sciences, which has been conducted by some of the scholars in the group.

"By developing interdisciplinary collaborations with medicine and the health sciences, we are able to conduct research that will benefit citizens and help resolve societal problems, and meanwhile we are gaining more knowledge about the nature and possibilities of literature, which is very rewarding," says Anne-Marie Mai.

The scholars working specifically with the methods and practice of interdisciplinary research are driven by curiosity and openness towards the possibilities for innovation of academia – they are also, however, aware of the risks involved in experimenting with crossing the boundaries of the disciplines.

Klaus Petersen, professor in both history and political science, points out that the cross-disciplinary discussions and work undertaken is the culmination of cooperation over several years and mutual interest in similar topics:

"Cross-disciplinarity is very challenging for the involved researchers. We are all products of disciplinary traditions and boundaries. However, with the Uses of Literature project we were able to push ourselves to challenge these boundaries. A lot of the topics studied in the group – such as state-citizen relationships, precarity and marginalized groups, or inequality – are key topics both within the social sciences, history and literature studies. Challenging each other and working together opens for new insights," Petersen says. His judgment is that the project has been very ambitious and successful in this respect, as the scholars have built an environment of mutual trust and understanding, which means they have managed to create work that is truly interdisciplinary on a deep, systematic level – rather than merely adding to each other's work: "We have

Group photo of some of the Uses of Literature researchers at the coastline in Nyborg, May 2017. Left to right: Klaus Petersen, Anne-Marie Mai, Lars Handesten, Paul Marx, Bryan Yazell, Moritz Schramm, Anne-Marie Søndergaard Christensen, Jon Helt Haarder, Rita Felski, Anders Juhl Rasmussen, Alastair Morrison, Patrick Fessenbecker, Emily Hogg, Mathies Græsborg Aarhus, Marie-Elisabeth lei Holm, Heidi Vad Jønsson, Peter Simonsen, Pernille Hasselsteen, Johanne Gormsen Schmidt and Camilla Schwarz
Photo: David Binzer

taken this to a higher level than is usually the case. This becomes very clear when looking at both the process and the output in terms of publications and new projects. And this has attracted a lot of attention internationally."

In September 2020, the Uses of Literature group organized the web-seminar *Thinking like a Sociologist: Theories, Methods, and Risks*, which explored the possibilities, challenges and limits of applying or engaging with sociological theories and methods – and what literature and literary critics can offer social scientists. They have also organized a number of workshops on cross-disciplinarity with researchers from the Uses of Literature project and other interested scholars at SDU.

In the fall of 2020, Rita Felski organized the first talks of the online series *Forms of Reading,* which continued in 2021. The first presentations were given by James English (professor at University of Pennsylvania) and Associate professor Elaine Auyoung (University of Minnesota) about the relations between literary studies and other disciplines among a number of topics.

Literature and social scientists

Klaus Petersen, Bryan Yazell, Patrick Fessenbecker, and Paul Marx have collaborated extensively on exploring and describing the uses of literature in connection with other disciplines. Petersen is Professor of History at SDU and part of the organizing group behind Uses of Literature, Yazell is an Assistant Professor at the department for the Study of Culture and research fellow at the Danish Institute for Advanced Studies at SDU, Fessenbecker was a postdoc at SDU and now Associate Professor at Bilkent University, Ankara, Marx was an associate professor in political science at SDU and now professor of political science and socio-economics at the University of Duisburg-Essen.

In their article *The role of literary fiction in facilitating social science research,* which was published in the journal *Humanities & Social Sciences Communications,* the four academics investigate "the ways social scientists might draw influence from literary fiction in the development of their own work as academics: selecting research topics, teaching, and drawing inspiration for projects." As part of the study, they sent a qualitative survey to 13.784 social science researchers at 25 different universities and received 875 responses.

Rather than focusing solely on how literature was mentioned in academic journals, the scholars investigated how the social scientists were influenced by literature before and during their work process, in order to create a fuller image of the role of literature. Thus, the survey asked them to elaborate on the various ways literary fiction has factored into their research, education, and day-to-day work.

The study presents several interesting findings. For example, almost half of the scientists reported that literary works had played important roles in their own work. Furthermore, the study points out three findings that could be further investigated:

"First, the survey reveals a skepticism among early-career researchers regarding literature's social insights compared to their more senior colleagues. Second, a significant number of respondents recognized literary fiction as playing some part in shaping their research interests and expanding their comprehension of subjects relevant to their academic scholarship. Finally, the survey generated a list of literary fiction authors and texts that respondents acknowledged as especially useful for understanding topics relevant to the study of the social sciences," Yazell, Petersen, Marx and Fessenbecker write in the article.

They hope that the article will help expand the picture of how disciplines that are adjacent to the study of literature esteem the value of fiction, and see it as a window into deeper learning and understanding of society.

"By asking these social scientists, we have found that literature in fact has had a formative impact on them. For some, literature has sparked an interest in a research topic or stimulated certain research questions. For others, literature has sharpened their curiosity," Petersen says.

He elaborates, that one of the most interesting aspects of conducting the study was to experience the high level of interest among the scientists to discuss the topic. Many participants wrote long replies to the survey's open questions and some even sent emails to Petersen and his colleagues in order to discuss the topic further or share their acknowledgement of the research topic.

This is the third article the scholars have co-authored on the topic, and it builds on the ideas and methodologies they have developed over time. In the essay *Idea, inspiration or illustration – when social science uses literature,* which is published in the anthology *Litteratur i brug (Use of Literature),* the scholars discuss whether and how social scientists use literature in their scholarly work, and attempt to develop a method to gather empirical data on the topic.

The Ethics of Belief

There have been several interdisciplinary projects across different academic fields and topics. Another collaboration Fessenbecker has participated in – and greatly benefitted from – is the one with Nikolaj Nottelmann, who is an Associate Professor of Philosophy at SDU. Together, they have written the article *Honesty and Inquiry: W.K. Clifford's ethics of belief,* published in *British Journal for the History of Philosophy* and the book chapter *The Conscience after Darwin*, which is part of the anthology *After Darwin*, published by Cambridge University Press.

In their article on W.K. Clifford's writings, Fessenbecker and Nottelmann offer alternative interpretations of the English philosopher's ethics of belief. They argue, that Clifford's position on the matter was in fact more complex than what is often believed. "Against Matthew Arnold's theory, where culture is the legacy of great artworks and morally useful doctrines, Clifford poses a theory of culture as the repository of shared true beliefs," Fessenbecker argues. "Each of us participates in this process of belief formation – we cannot help but do it – and we have a duty to participate well. And as we conclude by saying that this view is especially worth reconsidering today: in a world of widespread and dangerous conspiracy theorizing our duty to each other to believe well is vital".

According to Fessenbecker, the collaboration between scholars of literature or cultural studies and philosophy is incredibly giving, as they complement each other well in a case like this. Whereas philosophers are excellent at explaining and clarifying the ideas presented in a book, cultural critics "can see the effects of ideas broadly across a culture".

"Nottelmann had the argumentative instincts to think out the philosophical implications of all of Clifford's different ideas, where I had the background in the history of nineteenth-century England to see how Clifford was participating in a broad debate about what exactly constitutes a 'culture.' And there is a real opportunity to use this combined interpretive method to approach the works of literary authors, since by virtue of seeming 'literary' many great thinkers have never received the close and creative reconstruction at which philosophers excel," Fessenbecker argues.

Klaus Petersen and Alastair Morrison at a Uses of Literature seminar in Nyborg, May 2017. Photo: David Binzer

Reading Ideas

During his participation in Uses of Literature, Fessenbecker has finished his book *Reading Ideas In Victorian Literature: Literary Content as Artistic Experience*, which was published in 2020 from Edinburgh University Press, and was very influenced by the thoughts discussed at SDU, particularly Rita Felski's.

"In *Reading Ideas*, my main goal was to review a large body of literary theory and criticism and argue that undergirding the practice was a significant principle about what the point of literary criticism is: namely, the critic paraphrases the work of art to show that it advocates some set of interesting ideas. This theory of criticism has never been openly defended or even really clearly articulated; what is much more common is for a critic to claim that her analysis of a work's ideas stems from the proper grasp of the work's form," Fessenbecker explains. *Reading ideas* aims to close the gap between reading practice and literary theory, by understanding how critics have come to increasingly focus on form rather than content in their readings, and Fessenbecker underlines the value of addressing the content itself and not creating false boundaries between author and critic, literature and philosophy.

Fessenbecker builds on these ideas in the major project that he began working on during Uses of Literature, called *Truth as Beauty: Literature and the Future of Interpretation*, in which he reflects further on the concept of truth in literature – and with the first encounter with an exciting idea as an aesthetic experience. This work is highly influenced by the work of Rita Felski, as well as the discussions in the Uses of Literature group.

"The main insight the project gave is one that plays a central role in Rita Felski's *Hooked*: social structures and practices may mediate our relationship with works of art, but that does not mean they are solely responsible for creating it. Instead they are what permit it to appear. Aesthetic value and aesthetic experience need not be thought of as necessarily opposed to sociological explanations of the rise and fall of works of art: there is a way of doing sociology of literature –Rita's, but also Antoine Hennion's – that treats works of arts as themselves causal agents in the networks in which the phenomenological events we know as 'aesthetic experience' occur," Fessenbecker explains.

Patrick Fessenbecker and Emily Hogg, Taken at the Uses of Literature seminar i Nyborg, May 2017. Photo: David Binzer

New approaches to teaching

As the scholars have been thinking, writing and conducting research in new ways, they have begun thinking about the implications this will have on their teaching as a consequence. Therefore, pedagogy have more recently become a focus area, and they are now in the midst of a renewal of their teaching methods and material.

Inspired by Rita Felski's thoughts on context in *The Limits of Critique,* the researchers have looked particularly on the ways they present literary history to the students. While chronology has traditionally been the common way of presenting the development of literary works through time, they are now attempting to do things differently.

From 2017 and 2018 Peter Simonsen initiated a comprehensive, full scale reform of the teaching of literature in the English Department at both the BA and MA level, which was assisted by Emily Hogg and Anita Wohlmann, in particular. The reform has changed the teaching's emphasis on traditional, national literary history conceived of in terms of chronology to including questions of contemporary relevance, applicability and "uses" beyond the confines of literary studies themselves. This is an attempt to open and broaden the concept of "literature" as well as a rethinking of how to ask students to report on their learning in new formats and more concrete settings of use.

In the anthology *Læsninger på tværs (Criss-cross readings)*, which is edited by Camilla Schwartz, Lars Handesten and Jon Helt Haarder from Uses of Literature, canonical works have been coupled with contemporary texts in thematic chapters such as anxiety, love, ghettos and gardening in order to create connections across time. The anthology collects contributions from many literary scholars:

"We have gathered a great line-up of scholars from all Danish universities, and we hope that the book will find its way to the curriculum of all Danish university studies, thus channeling some of the insights from Uses of Literature concerning literary history into the teaching of literature," says Camilla Schwartz, Associate Professor in Danish literature at SDU.

There are several aims with the anthology. Firstly, the idea of literary history as a neat line of causes and effects has been questioned for decades and this questioning needs to be reflected in the ways in which literary history is taught. Secondly, students struggle to make sense of literary history by memorizing years and putting works onto a timeline. Thirdly, taking contemporary fiction as a gateway to older classics, scholars can make it easier for young students to enter them. So, through the thematic approach, they hope to help students create connections between texts that are written at different moments in time but revolve around the same issues or feelings and thereby making it more relevant.

In line with Felski and Latour, Handesten, Haarder and Schwartz want to emphasize the role of literary texts as agents that can carry meaning across time and reveal new insights by being read in relation to texts from other periods. In the book, they connect Edith Södergran with Michael Strunge, Amalie Skram with Cecilie Lind among others.

Several of the scholars who have participated in the Uses of Literature project mention how they have changed their approach to teaching. The concepts of attachment and recognition have opened for new ways of engaging with the texts. This does not mean that the students should leave close readings, critical thinking and analyzes behind, rather it should be seen as an additional way of approaching a text, meaning that the scholars will *also* ask their students to reflect upon their own feelings and reactions to a text.

Anne-Marie Mai builds on the same principles in her 2022 monograph *Litteraturland (Land of Literature),* where she seeks to engage the reader or student by suggesting new ways they can bring their own reading experiences into play, by for instance writing a portrait of themselves as readers and tracing the many actors that have influenced their own relationship with books. *Litteraturland* is rather untraditional, as it contains both writing exercises, essays as well as introductions to authors and texts. Furthermore, Mai has published two volumes on literary history inspired by Latour's actor-network theory; *Danish literature of the 20th and 21st century*, published in 2016, and *Danish literature from 1000 to 1900*, published in 2022.

Researchers who have been part of the work package on New Work in Literary Theory:

Anders Juhl Rasmussen
Anita Wohlmann
Anne-Marie Mai
Bryan Yazell
Camilla Schwartz
Elin Abrahamsson
Emily Hogg
Jon Helt Haarder
Marie-Elisabeth Lei Holm
Moritz Schramm
Peter Simonsen
Rita Felski
Sophy Kohler

Researchers who have been part of the work package on New Approaches to Contemporary Literature:

Anne-Marie Mai
Camilla Schwartz
Elin Abrahamsson
Johanne Gormsen Schmidt
Jon Helt Haarder
Lars Handesten
Mathies Græsborg Aarhus
Moritz Schramm
Nicklas Freisleben Lund
Peter Simonsen
Troels Obbekær

Researchers who have been part of the work package on Interdisciplinarity:

Anders Juhl Rasmussen
Anne-Marie Søndergaard Christensen
Bryan Yazell
Ella Fegitz
Emily Hogg
Heidi Vad Jønsson
Klaus Petersen
Paul Marx
Rita Felski
Sophy Kohler

Researchers who have been part of the work package for Young Researchers, The PhD Club

Anne-Marie Mai was leader of the group
Johanne Gormsen Schmidt
Marie-Elisabeth Lei Holm
Mathies Græsborg Aarhus
Sophy Kohler

Pernille Hasselsteen,
cand.mag, has been Project Manager of Uses of Literature.

Class, Precarity and the Social Dimensions of Literature

The topical term *precariat* has gained attention and contributed to renewed discussions of class, and a group of scholars from Uses of Literature have dedicated years of research to understand the implications of class as they look today. To put it briefly, *precariat* covers a growing group of people living under insecure and vulnerable conditions in the current neoliberal society; according to how the concept has been defined and described by scholars such as Pierre Bourdieu, Judith Butler and Guy Standing. The precariat covers diverse groups of people: some are long term unemployed, some suffer from chronic illnesses, some struggle with short term contracts and freelance work, others are migrants or refugees. People within this umbrella of the precariat are precarious in different ways and for different reasons, but have their struggle and their outsider position in common. Even so, they are rarely able to unite in political debates. Precarious conditions have always been a reality, but what is special about being precarious today, is that welfare states in earlier decades were more willing to protect their citizens through social security, unemployment benefits and pensions.

However, the scholars have not only investigated the working class, but also the middle class, those who are in-between classes, and various types of precarious classes. With an aim to "investigate class in its many facets with a focus on new theories exploring the relationship between class, cultural production, social formation and personal identities" the group of scholars has covered a wide range of issues: from unemployment in the 1930s, climate refugees in science fiction novels, voices from the so-called Danish ghetto in the 2010s, and much more.

The scholars working on topics related to class, precarity and the social dimensions of literature have held weekly meetings in order to share and develop their ideas, which has led to several co-authored papers, anthologies and monographs – as well as conference panels, and online seminars such as *"Estate Aesthetics: Social Housing and the Social Dimensions of Art and Literature"* which was based on a co-authored article about the British council estates, and *Nordisk Arbejderlitteratur VII Internationale perspektiver og forbindelser.*

After five years of research as part of the Uses of Literature project, the list of publications is long and still growing. Much of the research conducted as part of the project is either published or under publication in some of the best international and national journals and publishers in literary studies, such as *Textual Practice*, *Criticism*, *Contemporary Literature*, *Scandinavica*, *Edda*, *K&K*, *Bloomsbury*, *Spring,* and *Gyldendal*. Furthermore, the research has also found its way to journals outside the field of literary studies, such as *Tidsskrift for arbejdsliv*, *The Social History of Alcohol and Drugs* and the historical journal *Arbejderhistorie*.

Over two days in September 2018, the researchers organized the workshop *The Precariat in Art and Culture*, which was attended by scholars from Denmark, Belgium, Sweden, Norway, the UK and the US.

The anthology *Precarity in Contemporary Literature and Culture,* which was published in 2021 by *Bloomsbury*, is one of the major results of the group's joint efforts. It is edited by Professor Peter Simonsen and Associate Professor Emily Hogg and contains chapters from several members of the Uses of Literature group, as well as other prominent researchers in the field.

As a whole, the book argues that "vulnerability and insecurity, as they are experienced at work, in lack of access to state benefits and health care, in housing crises, and in brutal anti-migration policies, are central topics in the contemporary moment, and require urgent investigation. Secondly, it proposes that literary, cultural and artistic texts can be crucial resources for thinking through these issues," Hogg explains.

The precariat on the literary agenda

Since the 1970s, literary criticism has largely failed to confront questions about class as well as social and economic inequality, according to Peter Simonsen, Professor of European Literature at SDU. While it has been positive to witness the emergence of debates on topics such as gender, ethnic identity and discrimination,

Emily Hogg, September 2018. Photo: David Binzer

he argues that the issues concerning class and inequality have been unduly overlooked in the humanities.

"There has been a widespread idea that class was no longer an issue, that everyone is just different types of middle class now," Simonsen says. "But, in reality, inequality has increased globally. We have witnessed ever-growing precarious classes and a lack of communication and understanding across social classes."

Simonsen and his colleagues are interested in the relationship between literature and class, as well as in new concepts of class and new social stratifications, as they believe there is immense potential in looking at literature from both an interdisciplinary perspective *and* by taking literature seriously as an actor that both reacts to and shapes the surrounding society.

"We have put the precariat on the agenda for literary studies and opened the study of social class, social exclusion and social suffering to new approaches through a different hermeneutics than the automatically very skeptical one, that critics would typically adhere to when dealing with the question of 'literature and society.'

Instead we have worked with a hermeneutics that is more aligned with Rita Felski's project in her trilogy of studies that culminated with *Hooked*," Simonsen says. "This potentially means that scholars and people beyond the academy, traditionally uninterested in the links between aesthetics and politics, may become engaged or at least aware of the human consequences of rising social inequality at the present time."

Speaking for the abandoned precariat

Simonsen sees an enormous gap between the middle class and the precarious class, but also a lack of understanding between different groups within the precariat. These divides between people from different social spheres are well-represented in works by Danish authors such as Morten Pape, Kristian Bang Foss, Yahya Hassan and Madame Nielsen, that all contain sharp descriptions of social inequality.

Together with his colleagues Camilla Schwartz and Jon Helt Haarder, Simonsen has co-written the article *Hvem kan tale for prekariatet – og hvorfra? (Who can speak for the precariat – and where from?)*, which has been published in the leading Scandinavian journal for literary studies, *Edda*. As of October 2021, the article has been downloaded through the PURE system app 400 times. It analyzes how the precariat is represented in four texts of contemporary Danish literature and in a documentary TV show from the Danish Broadcasting Corporation and in particular, the scholars focus on questions of narrative point of view, recognition, and representation, as they investigate these five portrayals of life in social housing estates.

An interesting paradox plays a role in their analysis, because even though the writers (as well as their narrators) are originally *from* the precariat, they speak from positions where they have either left the precariat and travelled upwards to the middle class, or find themselves in a fragile hybrid state between the two. Thus, Haarder, Simonsen and Schwartz found a "detachment from the ghetto as place, and from life as precarious". The scholars conclude that these complicated narrative positions imply that society might put less emphasis on shared culture or class and more on recogniz-

Peter Simonsen, at a Uses of Literature seminar in Nyborg – May 2017
Photo: David Binzer

ing and increasingly understanding differences, if we are to create a greater sense of solidarity across classes.

"As scholars, we can work on how literature can be used in order to create a nuanced understanding of class divides across Denmark, as well as internationally. There are immense prejudices and gaps of understanding which we believe that literature and literary research can counter, and that is something very meaningful to work on," Simonsen says.

Helle Helle's perspective on the precarious
The popular author Helle Helle has been awarded recognition and numerous prizes for her works. However, she has often been read as apolitical by critics and readers. In many cases, she is seen as having a lack of awareness of political issues or social struggles.

Simonsen disagrees. He argues that Helle's books can be read as works that are very aware of social and economic conditions, which he elaborates on in *Prekarisering og prekært arbejdsliv i Helle*

Helles roman Ned til hundene (*Precarization and precarious work life in Helle Helle's novel Down to the Dogs*), which has been published in *Tidsskrift for arbejdsliv*, a journal on working conditions.

Simonsen argues that in fact, Helle often portrays people who are without representation, who lack a voice to express their struggles and needs, and as a result, get little attention in the current Danish welfare state. In the article, Simonsen lists some of the jobs of the essential characters in Helle's books, and what all of the characters have in common is that they are precarious in various ways.

Moreover, the narrators in Helle's books are mostly unreliable and unable to understand their surroundings, themselves or other people: This is described in a precise, sober language where details are observed but never analyzed, and many things are left unsaid. This style of writing, which Simonsen suggests can be dubbed a "precarious narration", leaves space for the reader's reflections on the characters' relationships and conditions. In this sense, Helle shows fragments of precarious peoples' lives without presenting statements or conclusions about them.

In his article, Simonsen analyzes Helle's 2008 novel *Ned til Hundene*, where an unreliable middle-class narrator arrives in a small town and becomes acquainted with three characters who are suffering from their injuries after a serious car accident. They all struggle with problem such as loss of a family member, mental health issues, illnesses, and precarious short-term work.

In Simonsen's reading of the text, the narrator is intentionally portrayed as having little understanding for neither the complexities of the people she meets, nor the high-level of stress and insecurity they are facing in their daily lives. He describes how the narrator mirrors the reader's own middle-class perspective on these precarious people, and the lack of empathy and respect towards them, which eventually leads to abuses of their trust. This situation can be seen as a parallel to the greater dynamics between the different classes in society today:

"The literary work of art becomes a reminder of the limits of our understanding and the consequences of our prejudice," Simonsen writes.

Theater of the precariat

The article *Theater of the Precariat: Staging Precarity in Alexander Zeldin's Love,* co-authored by Peter Simonsen and his fellow researcher Mathies Græsborg Aarhus (who completed his PhD under the auspices of the Uses of Literature project) has won international recognition. The article has been published in the renowned journal *Contemporary Literature* and won the L. S. Dembo Prize for the best article published in *CL* in Volume 61.

The article looks at what Simonsen and Aarhus call the "Theatre of the Precariat" as it has been expressed in Alexander Zeldin's play *Love,* as well as in four recent British plays. The scholars argue that recognition is essential in order to improve the conditions of the precariat, and that theatrical plays can act as strong mediums for recognition, as plays are performed live with real people onstage (and sometimes even including people from the audience in the performance), so they have the potential to hold attention and create strong impressions and responses among the people watching.

Love features a diverse range of characters such as a Muslim migrant, a pregnant student, an incontinent elderly person, and many unemployed people – all of whom can be viewed as vulnerable and part of the diverse class of the precariat today. However, Zeldin does not refer to the work as being *political*. Rather, he aims to touch his audience, which, according to the scholars, has the potential to expand their perspective and understanding of other peoples' struggles.

"The contemporary theater of the precariat is reluctant to be prescriptive, or offering political solutions, preferring instead to give the audience a glimpse into the suffering on and off the stage," Simonsen and Aarhus write.

From the industrial slaughterhouse to the privileged precariat

The definition of the precariat is an issue that can cause great debate, as it covers an extremely diverse group of people. Nicklas Freisleben Lund is a postdoc at the Danish Aging Research Center (DARC), but besides his research in literary representations of aging, he has an

Group photo of a part of the Uses of Literature group and Mads Rosendahl Thomsen, taken at the Uses of Literature seminar in Svendborg, May 2019. From left to right: Anita Wohlmann, Anne-Marie Mai, Jon Helt Haarder, Anders Juhl Rasmussen, Mathies Græsborg Aarhus, Johanne Gormsen Schmidt, Bryan Yazell, Alastair Morrison, Camilla Schwartz, Anne-Marie Søndergaard Christensen, Moritz Schramm, Nickals Freisleben Lund, Emily Hogg, Sophy Kohler, Mads Rosendahl Thomsen, Marie-Elisabeth Lei Holm, Lars Handesten, Patrick Fessenbecker, Rita Felski, Peter Simonsen and Pernille Hasselsteen. Photo: David Binzer

interest in working class literature, how it has developed, and how precarious conditions are portrayed in contemporary literature, which he describes in the book chapter *Towards the Light, Into the Silence: Danish Working-Class Literature Past and, Perhaps, Present*, which was published in the anthology *Working-class literature(s): Historical and international perspectives*.

In his PhD dissertation *I ambivalent kamp: Strejken og romanen, 1850-1950 (In ambivalent struggle: The strike and the novel 1850-1950)*, Lund investigated the role of strikes in literary history – the dissertation was awarded Arbejderhistorieprisen in 2019, which is given to the best work on Danish or international working class history each year. In relation to this topic, Lund has become interested in how the precariat is part of a new lower-class that is more diverse than the traditional working-class. As a result, the literary depictions of this class are equally diverse. In a Danish context, the genre of traditional working class literature occurred around 1870 and is generally thought to disappear around 1980. However, Lund argues, depictions of life on the margins of society simply take another shape today, and can thus be considered a form of continuity of the traditions, and in recent years an increasing number of texts focusing on class, inequality, social segregation and work have been published.

"We sometimes tend to forget that there are people working under conditions different from our own", but a book such as Kenneth Jensen's *Tragedie plus tid*, can act as a reminder of the working conditions at an industrial slaughterhouse, and draw attention to circumstances that we are otherwise unaware of," says Lund.

This is exactly one of the things that literature can do: create a deeper understanding of how other people experience life that you cannot get from reading an economic report with statistics of unemployment or living conditions. By communicating lived experiences, providing the reader with images and sensuous descriptions, we can gain another form of thinking.

In his article *Privileged Precarity and Precarious Class Solidarity*, Lund analyzes the representations of precarity in the Danish author Nikolaj Zeuthen's novel *Buemundet guitarfisk* (*Bowmouth Guitarfish*) that depicts a poet and former scholar falling into precarity.

"If *Buemundet guitarfisk* is a novel highly engaged in the question of precarity and a novel markedly different from the existing Danish precarious literature, it is because it extrapolates the experience of precarious existence among the more privileged demographics of Standing's class-in-the-making," Lund writes in the article.

"Thus, when we are talking about the precariat, we are talking about the refugee and the freelance journalist, the long-time unemployed unskilled worker and the graphic designer relying on social benefits between projects, the temporary cleaner and the part-time lecturer. All of these might share characteristics concerning levels of income and modes of employment. But in regard to social and cultural resources, lifestyle and life expectations they are likely to differ significantly."

The novel depicts the "increased economic and social insecurity experienced by the protagonist," but it presents another form of precarity that differs significantly from the conditions refugees or vulnerable working-class people face. Historically, the call for solidarity has been an integral part of working class literature, but the message seems more opaque in a work of fiction such as Zeuthen's, which presents a protagonist who never seems to be satisfied:

"Zeuthen's precarious comedy raises a different question, which the novel itself indeed does not answer. How and to what extent can we feel solidarity with the privileged precariat? That is, how can we feel solidarity with those who in many regards have a lot – and demand even more – but are nonetheless affected by processes of becoming precarious?" writes Lund.

Reassembling the Ghetto

Jon Helt Haarder is Associate Professor of Literature and has a special relationship with the so-called Danish ghetto, where he happily lived for years before moving on to living in typical upper-middle class homes. As a result of his participation in the Uses of Literature group – and in particular his discussions with colleagues about literature relating to precarity – he found inspiration to explore this familiar concept of the ghetto as part of his academic work.

"Walking down the corridor after a meeting one day, it dawned on me that not only does social segregation have everything to do with geography, but also that I myself spent my first 10 years in various concrete blocks on the southern outskirts of Aarhus," Haarder writes. "Here was a subject very much related to *The Social Dimensions of Literature*, but also directly to my own life."

In May 2021, he received funding from the Danish Research Foundation for the three-year project, which he has named *Reassembling the Ghetto*. Haarder underlines that the application and its success would have been "unthinkable" without his participation in Uses of Literature and the support and feedback from his colleagues in the group.

In the new project, Haarder plans to write a monograph, as well as articles and conference papers on the literary representation of how the Danish ghetto has developed over time. The project will examine how literature can be used in order to create a more nuanced understanding of class divisions, which will build upon research that Haarder has already conducted on the topic as part of Uses of Literature.

"I want to tell the stories of how these housing areas have developed into the opposite of what they were intended to be. They represent a history of Denmark, a literary history, as well as my own personal story," Haarder said.

Historically, the view on the concrete buildings – that are now referred to as ghettos – have changed dramatically. When they were first planned and built in the 1960s, the housing estates were seen as manifestations of the ideal living area, where people from the middle and working classes could meet and enjoy their leisure time in the common areas. During the 1970s, however, the very same areas became symbols of everything that was felt to be wrong in Denmark, as it became a multicultural, yet clearly divided, society. During the last couple of decades, some of them have been increasingly problematic and connected to social problems, unrest, and failed integration of citizens from non-European countries.

"Most of the residents living in these housing areas are citizens who simply live their lives without causing any trouble," Haarder explains. "But there are a few of these areas where violence and unrest is common, which has been reflected in literary fiction since 2010, and that is what my research is about; how these areas are depicted and how the texts relate to topics such as class, gender and ethnicity."

Gender has come to play a bigger role in the research project than Haarder had first planned, as he realized that class affiliations are performed in gendered ways that are specific to each class. Furthermore, he is interested in the role of the different types of fathers that are portrayed in literature about the ghettos.

Haarder hopes that within his project he will be able to provide a scientific footing for a different way of approaching and speaking about the so-called Danish ghettos.

"I believe that there is strong societal relevance in telling the stories from the concrete blocks as they appear in literature."

Bad vibes in the buildings

The term *ghetto* is a problematic one, which Haarder is very aware of. But since *ghetto* is the word that is used most frequently to describe precarious housing areas in current Danish debates by authors, politicians as well as the general public, this is the term Haarder has chosen to use. In his article *The Precariat as Place, a Literary History of the Danish Ghetto*, he closely interprets the historical backgrounds and changing meanings of the term and its use in a specifically Danish context:

"On par with many other agents such as concrete, housing policy, and inhabitants, literary texts are active in the assemblages that make up Danish ghettoes," writes Haarder. "The literary history I am charting here is an aspect of the complex dynamics between estates, welfare society, and cultural products such as literature that have assigned this particular kind of housing area a specific location on the map of contemporary Danish class society."

In the article, Haarder conducts readings of authors such as Anders Bodelsen, Jonas T. Bengtsson, Geeti Amiri, Tarek Omar and Tage Skou-Hansen in order to analyze how they describe geographical representations of class and identity. In a reading of Bent Haller's novel *Katamaranen (The Catamaran)* from 1976, Haarder concludes:

"Even if the novel as a whole places the reality of the tough neighborhood in a larger context, quotes such as this one seem to suggest that the bad vibes emanate from the buildings themselves, and thus that the problems in the area have their roots in the area and the buildings themselves. This determinism is a form of territorialiszation and a drift that runs contrary to the explicit intention of the novel: protesting against the spatial segregation taking place in the mid 1970s that turned a Danish estate into a local articulation of Danish class society."

The ghetto as portrayed in hip hop

In addition to Haarder's own research, the project has engaged Troels Obbekær as a PhD student, who will explore the literary representations of the ghetto through selected works of Danish hip hop music. Since the genre is very popular in these environments, it is an essential manifestation of the class and gender identities

A part of the Uses of Literature group at the Uses of Literature seminar in Nyborg, May 2017. From left to right: Moritz Schramm, Anne-Marie Søndergaard Christensen, Anders Juhl Rasmussen, Alastair Morrison, Patrick Fessenbecker, Rita Felski, Klaus Petersen, Emily Hogg, Jon Helt Haarder, Anne-Marie Mai, Peter Simonsen, Paul Marx, Marie-Elisabeth Lei Holm, Heidi Vad Jønsson, Johanne Gormsen Schmidt, Mathies Græsborg Aarhus, Camilla Schwartz, Lars Handesten, Bryan Yazell and Pernille Hasselsteen. Photo: David Binzer

that are performed in these particular places. Haarder argues that hip hop must be taken seriously in its own right when analyzing representations of the ghetto, as it is a verbal form of art which is extremely dynamic and evolves more quickly than literary fiction.

Haarder credits Rita Felski's thinking for influencing his approach and making it more inclusive of different literary expressions and the relationships with their users and environment. Felski's work has created a solid theoretical foundation for looking at how readers and listeners interact with, relate to, and become attached to artworks.

"In order for art to be alive, there needs to be someone who sees, reads and listens to it; that is where the art emerges. As scholars, of course we are working scientifically, but we must remember the sensuous qualities of literature and its ability to open our worlds," Haarder says.

Unemployment and affect

When postdoc Mathies Græsborg Aarhus investigates the representations of unemployment in literary fiction, the darker aspects of human existence are at the forefront of his research. In 2020, he defended his PhD dissertation *The Idle Feel*, which explores the changing emotions connected to unemployment as described in selected literature from the 1930s until today.

In *The Idle Feel*, Aarhus focuses on the painful feelings attached to unemployment and how the reactions to feeling socially inferior are expressed differently through time. While the low status of the unemployed has been consistent over time, feelings connected to the experience have changed, which Aarhus substantiates in his analyzes of eight literary works.

"The dissertation argues that whereas the social suffering of unemployment was connected to resentment and apathy during the Great Depression, it is now attached to specific forms of anxiety, shame and nostalgia. The recent anxious feeling surrounding unemployment is partly due to the precarization of labor brought on by neoliberalism and the essentially downward distribution of precarity at our present moment," Aarhus explains. "Further, unemployment increasingly attaches itself to shame because of recent labor market and governmental demands, which dictate that the unemployed are failing as selves, rather than as workers, because they are unable to develop the desired emotional dispositions."

In other words: our contemporary society values work and productivity above all else. And if you are not a "contributing" member of society, there is something to be ashamed of.

Aarhus argues that in the 1930s, the dominant feeling around unemployment was anger. In Walter Greenwood's *Love on the Dole* from 1933, which was extremely popular at the time of its publication and is among the most well known British books about unemployment, feelings of resentment are strong. Not only does the book depict the personal consequences of unemployment, it also deals with the structural injustices within the British social system at the time.

Since the 1930s, the emotional responses to the condition change character in the literary representations:

"When the British and American welfare states were experiencing reform in the 1980s, the unemployment novels changed character, and the predominant emotion found in the literature is anxiety rather than anger," says Aarhus.

James Kelman *How Late it Was, How Late* is an emblematic book from the period. Written in 1994, the feeling of anxiousness is present as a theme. The form mirrors this emotional state, as the reader follows the narrator, a blind man who has been unemployed for several years, as he wanders nervously around Glasgow.

In March 2019, Aarhus arranged a panel at the ACLA (American Comparative Literature Association) Conference in collaboration with PhD student Taylor Johnston from the University of California, Berkeley on Affects and Class, which was directly related to his PhD research. Scholars from Europe as well as North America participated in the panel, which was very well attended and received.

The future of work

In current debates, unemployment is often portrayed as being shameful and problematic for the individual person, because productivity has become a core value in capitalist society. But our perspectives around careers, work and the loss of work are not only shaped by societal developments, our narratives are also very active in shaping what it means to be unemployed, Aarhus argues.

"As opposed to most economic and sociological approaches to class, this study speaks to the importance of culture as a vehicle for framing classed experiences like unemployment," he says. "Unemployment would not feel the way it does, I argue, if it was not framed in the way it is by culture. In other words, social agents – and here I include feelings – *do* things to class in the course of their everyday activities and engagements with the world."

Literature's imagination of emerging and future forms of work are into, themes that Aarhus has recently begun to look into and the research on the future of work is a continuation of the interests he acquired during his participation in the Uses of Literature project. In his new research, Aarhus seeks to investigate the cultural significance of work-related issues like unemployment, precarization and automation. In a recent article, he studies how the warehouse is represented in contemporary Danish and English literature as both a setting where modern work forms take place, and as an image of the precarious workers' conditions today.

The feminization of work

Emily Hogg began her time in the Uses of Literature group as an Assistant Professor, and was promoted to Associate Professor in 2021. In the past five years, she has been working on issues relating to various forms of precarity reflected in contemporary literature.

One of her most recent projects focuses on the way in which contemporary British and Irish literature reflects on alcohol and precarity in society. Hogg is currently working on a book that examines how literary texts connect representations of drinking and representations of the insecurity and vulnerability that is intensified by contemporary capitalism. Although many clichés and stereotypes associate problematic drinking with lower-class citizens of the two countries, the book focuses on the diverse, complex ways contemporary literature imagines alcohol consumption in relation to precarious lives. Beyond the stereotypical figure of the alcoholic homeless person or the binge-drinker spending state benefits on booze, the book shows how representations of drinking in situations of precarity generate new ways of understanding themes such as temporality, embodied experience and risk-taking.

In addition, Hogg examines the idea of the feminization of work in her current project, *Feminized: A New Literary History of Women's Work*, which has been funded by the Carlsberg Foundation. The term "feminization of work" refers to the fact that the working conditions that were formerly associated with women – such as informal work, short-term contracts, care work, emotional labor and work that takes place in the home – have become generalized across the labor market. The project will explore how 20th century global Anglophone writing can illuminate and explore this trend. Through three sub-projects, it will look at representations of women's work in literature from different global contexts, including British realist fiction and post-colonial African novels.

Anne-Marie Søndergaard Christensen on the left and Emily Hogg on the right. Seminar with Heather Love, June 2018. Photo: David Binzer

Hogg has two general aims with the project. The first is to generate new knowledge about so-called feminized work. The second is to explore the literary theoretical aspects of the project, which has to do with how scholars can interpret literature not only in its own historical context, and in the light of what was important when it was written, but how they can interpret literature across time. Hogg hopes to gain new insights into the way literary texts from the past can be used to provide distinctive insights into topical social and political issues in the present.

The issues of gender are not seen as isolated, but rather as an integrated parts of the issues related to economic precarity and class struggles. Hogg gives an example from the British context, where sectors that have traditionally been associated with men, such as heavy industry, have experienced increasing unemployment over the last 30 years. The jobs that are increasingly available today are service industry work and jobs that require high levels of communicative skills, which have often been considered "feminine".

"If we want to understand the landscape of how class operates today, we need to think of how that also involves gender, and the ideas of what 'the right type' of work is for a particular gender," Hogg said.

Through this project she hopes to develop the studies of contemporary work and literature with a specific focus on gender, in order to influence and challenge the ways scholars and people in general think about work. As part of the project, Hogg has been able to hire a PhD student, Ida Aaskov Dolmer, and a postdoc. She hopes to create a network for people who are interested in these relatively new research areas by organizing events and networks for national and international scholars.

The idea for the new project has been developed during the Uses of Literature project, and is, to a great degree, influenced by the discussions and thoughts on precarity and literature which Hogg has had with her fellow researchers at SDU.

The problems with "female empowerment"

Female empowerment is a buzzword in contemporary society, but the concept can in fact be problematic, according to postdoc Ella Fegitz, who joined the Uses of Literature group in 2019.

In her academic career, she has focused on the construction of post-feminist subjectivity in neo-liberal societies and its relation to media representations. She is interested in the role of especially elderly women in work and political life, as well as the ideas of "female empowerment".

Female empowerment today is problematic because, according to Fegitz, it is predominantly defined by work life; earning an income and being successful in a professional career.

"Work becomes the key way through which women can be empowered in society and culture," she says. "I think it is highly problematic because it reproduces work as key to fulfilment and reproduces a neoliberal understanding of society in the way in which it makes appealing an increasing responsibilization of the individual to look after themselves throughout their lives, and in old age."

This needs to be criticized for several reasons, she argues. Firstly, it creates a very narrow understanding of what it means for women to be "empowered" in a way that might not be beneficial for everyone, such as women who cannot work due to caring responsibilities.

Secondly, it creates an underlying societal opinion that everyone should be able to rely on themselves socially as well economically – but not everyone has the same abilities to take care of themselves throughout their lives. The worst outcome of the encouragement to work is that it naturally leads to the idea that everyone should take care of themselves in old age rather than relying on the state to provide care homes and health services.

"We forget how older people are actually being deeply impacted by neoliberal changes in society, such as changes to the pension system," Fegitz says, referring specially to the British context, where there have been attacks on the pension system alongside increasing responsibilization of life in old age.

Political affects in media and on TV

In her current research as part of Uses of Literature, Fegitz explores how older women are being included in contemporary culture by analyzing relevant British policies and media representations.

Fegitz is interested in aging femininity and work beyond the retirement age. Since September 2019, she has engaged in interdisciplinary research, exploring the discourses about aging entrepreneurial femininity in both popular culture and public policy. A new research interest is about automation in care for the elderly, and how UK public policy depicts automation in eldercare as a way to free older women from the "burden" of having to care for their even older relatives.

In the fall of 2021, Fegitz examined the television show *The Good Fight* and how depictions of emotions relate to particular feminist politics in the show. It became apparent how confusion and depression were portrayed as leading to political inactivity, while anger was depicted as an emotion from which political and collective action could arise. By mapping the emotions in the show and connecting them to wider culture and what happened in the aftermath of Trump's presidential election, Fegitz analyzed how *The Good Fight* connects with a specific progressive female audience.

"It is interesting that the main character in this show is a woman in her sixties," she remarks. "I am arguing that it marks a shift in our cultural understanding of age and femininity in the sense that older women have been invisible for such a long time in the media, and now we are beginning to see older women not only being represented but also becoming central to the narratives."

The approach to the research is inspired by Uses of Literature, which has had a great impact on how Fegitz works methodologically. Through discussions and interactions with her colleagues at SDU, she has become more open to looking at the relationships a text can create with the audiences and to doing participatory research in the future.

Creating images of vagrancy

There once was a time where a particular group of single white men were seen as the greatest threat to American democracy – they were called hobos and tramps. Charlie Chaplin's silent film, *The Tramp* was a famous and widely popular depiction of the character. When we close our eyes and think of someone that could be of danger to our society today, the white houseless man would probably not be the first thing that came to mind.

Bryan Yazell is an Assistant Professor at the department for the Study of Culture and research fellow at the Danish Institute for Advanced Studies at SDU, and has been part of the Uses of Literature group from its inception. One of his research interests is the changing representations of vagrancy and unemployment, and the ways that literary fiction can influence societal ideas and opinions about this group of people. Yazell has been working on a book called *Vagrant States: American Vagrancy Literature and Transatlantic Welfare Policy* during his time in the Uses of Literature research group, and among other things, he focuses on how cultural depictions of economic precarity relate to public opinion and policies.

"I argue that homelessness and unemployment have been problems in varying degrees forever, but that a new type of homeless person was created around the turn of the twentieth century," said Yazell. "The tramp or the hobo was a particular manifestation that seemed new and was intensely popular."

Yazell's project traces the development of this character, and shows how literature can engage and even take a lead in the public's understanding of something like a public policy issue.

He argues that literature and culture play important roles in politics, as they shape peoples' imagination and stereotypical ideas – so much so, that it can end up affecting legislators. Because of responsive governments and representational democracy, if the public has a fascination with or fear of a certain group, it can create the foundation for legislative change. Yazell has conducted research on John Steinbeck's books and their role in society in his lifetime. He is very interested in how popular literature can shape public opinion.

Steinbeck's 1939 novel *The Grapes of Wrath* is an interesting example of this dynamic, because the author had a clear agenda to improve the conditions for the poorest. He succeeded in influencing politicians to introduce new welfare measures by convincing a great number of readers that they should care for a particular group of vulnerable people. "I am interested in authors who were very popular in their lifetime, such as Mark Twain, George Orwell and Jack London, because I look at ideas of influence," says Yazell. "Steinbeck is the clearest example of a literary author who really helped drive public opinion around Dust Bowl farmers in a way that is still relevant today."

The book creates a longer timeline and context for the debates that are happening about migrants, houseless people, and refugees today. Yazell argues that these issues are ongoing historical conversations and that the discourse has stayed the same until now, even if current debates are often driven by recent events and focused on particular present conditions.

"By understanding some of the techniques government sources or populist politicians might use to describe immigrants, and knowing that they actually have a long history, you might be able to counter it better," Yazell says.

"This is also why I am interested in the idea of popular imaginations or receptions of precarious groups; because this is exactly the

Bryan Yazell in the front and Peter Simonsen in the background. The picture is taken at the Uses of Literature seminar in Nyborg, May 2017. Photo: David Binzer

problem we are getting at, that certain ideas or stereotypes circulate and become very profound and fixed," he says.

Yazell believes that it is important for scholars to address these issues, and by doing so, try and break them.

Science fiction and climate change

The issues of vagrancy and unemployment in popular literature led Yazell to look more closely at science fiction. It occurred to him that books within this genre often depict hoards of people on the move or permanently displaced and that vagrancy is an almost universal theme. It made him curious to take a closer look at how science fiction can illuminate a number of shared expectations (or fears) for the future.

As the genre is both extremely popular and deals with issues such as climate change and its possible consequences, it contains a powerful combination and has the potential to engage readers to take action against a societal challenge that can otherwise be difficult to grasp.

"It ties into the larger problem of climate change being one of these imaginative problems where people are told to expect it, yet it does not seem to break through at all. It is a topic that is difficult to visualize in popular media. It is often discussed politically – that displacement will be one of the major effects of climate change, as people will flee areas that are under water or suffering from long droughts, and that we are facing an immense number of climate refugees or migrants."

The term *imaginative failure* covers our inability to visualize and recognize the very real consequences that climate change has and will have in the future. The Indian novelist Amitav Ghosh has been one of the most prominent voices criticizing authors of contemporary literary fiction for their failure to depict the issue seriously. Ghosh is among those who argue that literature has the ability, as well as the responsibility, to portray the effects of climate change in ways that are more convincing than the media reports and warnings from experts have yet been.

In addition, there are debates about how literature can meaningfully engage with something like climate change, as it can be argued that by writing science fiction stories about climate change that take place in the future, authors could wrongfully give the impression that it is a problem that does not exist in the present.

"There is a long tradition of looking at science fiction as an escape from reality – an escape from everyday life – so there are debates about whether reading and writing science fiction reinforces the sense of escaping from social problems like climate change," explains Yazell.

Yazell is clearly on the side of the debate that says reading science fiction *really* engages with social problems in the present.

"The viability of good science fiction stories depends on how they engage with our own reality, by estranging our view of the world and creating a world that we recognize, but is just different enough that we still feel alienated, like foreigners in our own world," says Yazell. "And this foreign perspective is important for us in order to better scrutinize the world as it actually is."

In his article *A Sociology of Failure: Migration and Narrative Method in US Climate Fiction,* Yazell argues how "speculative climate fiction (or 'cli-fi') in the United States provides glimpses into how this social unrest might unfold by drawing from past and present precedents."

Yazell analyzes how popular science fiction novels such as Clara Vaye Watkins's *Gold Fame Citrus,* Paolo Bacigalupi's *The Water Knife,* and Kim Stanley Robinson's *New York 2140* represent ideas about the future consequences of climate change.

Even though these works all have characters that average American readers would be able to relate to – rather than characters from the Global South, who are already experiencing serious effects of climate change – Yazell argues that this approach can be useful in order to create identification, which leads to readers that engage more strongly with the issues presented in the stories.

"They together reflect a prevailing trend in popular examples of the genre: rather than enlarge their imaginative scope geographically and demographically, they narrow it," writes Yazell.

This might not be as problematic as it sounds, however, as the books can be effective in confronting their target audience with their own roles, ideas and responsibilities in relation to climate change. By making the readers question their own norms and opinions, the novels can ideally awaken a more critical way of thinking about their surroundings as well as a sensitivity towards the conditions that other people are already exposed to.

The topic is something that Yazell will explore further in a coming book project on sociology and climate fiction entitled *Imaginative Failure? How Literature Informs Public Perception of the Climate Crisis.* This book will build upon the approaches developed during the Uses of Literature project, such as rethinking the methods for evaluating the social impacts of literature.

A new language for migration literature
Questions related to migration have been studied from several different angles.

In her PhD dissertation, *Reading for Relation: Forms of Attachment in Comtemporary Migration Literature,* Sophy Kohler explores forms of attachment and its relation to contemporary migration literature through the following question: how can a focus on attachment enrich the field of migration studies and postcolonial criticism? The aim is to find a new language for talking about migration literature; one that draws on postcolonial literary theory and pushes beyond it, as it has tended to involve an emphasis on disconnections, rupture and people losing their sense of identity.

Kohler has been very inspired by Rita Felski's recent work *Hooked: Art and Attachment,* and she aims to use attachment to broaden the engagement with migration literature and extend the frameworks of migration studies and postcolonialism that are predominantly used in readings of the genre.

"The way we speak about migration is usually about people being dispossessed or feeling uprooted from their community, and I think what we see in the body of migration literature as a whole is that this is not always the stories that are being told," says Kohler. "So, I also emphasize the things that provide a continuity, a sense of grounding for people who migrate, who do not necessarily experience only the opposite."

The dissertation focuses on six works of literary fiction that explore different angles of migration. As an example, one chapter compares V. S. Naipaul's *The Enigma of Arrival* with Teju Cole's *Open City*, two works that are often mentioned together but have not received any sustained comparison in scholarly work.

"In *The Enigma of Arrival*, Naipaul is able to feel a sense of being at home when he moves from Trinidad to England, because he has a familiarity with the English landscape that comes from the British literature he studied under a colonial syllabus in Trinidad," Kohler says.

Attachment plays a key role in Kohler's approach to the material, as she draws on Felski's thoughts on attachment by looking at modes of relation between texts, through texts, as well as in the characters' relationship to the world around them, their relationships to objects and to people. Kohler argues that postcolonial theory cannot be avoided when dealing with migration studies, as the two fields have evolved together and are closely associated, so in order to intervene in one, it is necessary to engage with the other, too. Therefore, she attempts to engage in a productive dialogue between migration studies, postcolonial studies, and post-critical scholarship which is something that has not previously been done.

Precarity in South African literature

During her PhD studies at SDU, Kohler has taken part in the research group which examined issues related to class, precarity and the social dimensions of literature, and she became interested in applying the concept of precarity to South African literature. Knowing the societal situation and the literature very well, Kohler could see that it would be a meaningful and original topic for research.

"Coming from South Africa, which is a country with a high unemployment rate and a great degree of poverty and inequality, it struck me that theorizations of precarity, for example the work of Laurent Berlant, had not been used much in speaking about South African literature, and it seemed like something that was missing from the conversation that was taking place globally. People who had this very real experience of precarity had stories that were not being represented in the scholarship," Kohler says.

In the chapter *Death Knells and Dead Ends, Latent Futurity in Masande Ntshanga's The Reactive and Mohale Mashigo's Ghost Strain N*, which was published in the anthology *Precarity in Contemporary Literature and Culture,* Kohler applies the concept of precarity in her readings of the two texts. According to her, the two works even embody the term precarity as they use narratives about illness and infection to show the precarious condition of their characters.

"Both texts address precarity-as-disappointment under the metonym of illness – a specific, embodied and more graspable phenomenon largely unlinked from economic specificities," Kohler writes in the article.

Doing Class in Swedish Fiction

Uses of Literature have been visited by a number of scholars from other universities. Åsa Arping, Professor of Comparative Literature at the University of Gothenburg in Sweden, visited SDU from the fall of 2020 until the fall of 2021 and was very inspired by the discussions about class, precarity and the social dimensions of literature that she took part in during her stay. Arping is currently working on a project in comparative literature, *Doing class: Intersectional encounters in contemporary Swedish fiction,* which investigates how class is depicted in Swedish contemporary literature.

"It has been most interesting to share thoughts on how a phenomenon like class is made visible in fiction, and how the manifestations of class-coded behavior, as well as how writers depict it, may differ in different national contexts. Even though we all strive for a transnational theoretical focus, I have also benefited greatly from the recurring Nordic and Danish perspectives in the group," Arping says.

Her current project on class examines "how class is charged with new political meanings and aesthetic expression" with the aim of gaining a deeper knowledge of "the political role of art and post-industrial society's obscured images of class, as perceptions of work, identity, lifestyle and the welfare state are rapidly changing."

During her time at SDU, Arping has been highly impressed by the high level of collaboration with her fellow researchers as well as the many events with scholars from outside the university, which is something she will continue applying in her future work. In addition, Arping's research interests are not limited to class, and she is currently also interested in studying new approaches to pedagogy in literary studies, as well as different forms of historical use of literature.

"The time I have spent at UoL has also given me a lot of thoughts and inspiration regarding a forthcoming project about how literary classics are 'used' and re-actualized in different contexts and formats," Arping says.

Researchers who have been part of the work package on Class, Precarity and the Social Dimensions of Literature:

Anders Bo Rasmussen
Anne-Marie Mai
Anne-Marie Søndergaard Christensen
Åsa Arping
Bryan Yazell
Camilla Schwartz
Ella Fegitz
Emily Hogg
Heidi Vad Jønsson
Jon Helt Haarder
Klaus Petersen
Mathies Græsborg Aarhus
Moritz Schramm
Nicklas Freisleben Lund
Pernille Tanggard Andersen
Peter Simonsen
Rita Felski
Sophy Kohler
Troels Obbekjær

Narrative Medicine and Medical Humanities

Literature can open new emotional spaces between health professionals and their patients, according to researchers at the University of Southern Denmark (SDU). This happens in different ways: by strengthening a narrative skill in the health care professional to expand their ability to see the people they treat as humans with complex stories – and in the patient to better accept their health condition and live a full life. As part of the Uses of Literature project, researchers of narrative medicine at SDU have explored various methods and theories within this emerging field. As a result, they have developed innovative seminars for students within the health care education system, conducted research on shared reading and creative writing workshops for ill and vulnerable citizens, established new academic networks, written a number of peer-reviewed articles, and edited anthologies.

Narrative medicine is a discipline that connects literary studies with the medical field, and is in its nature truly interdisciplinary. The research belongs under the umbrella of the growing field of Medical Humanities, which refers to the cooperation between the humanities, social sciences, and health sciences. It speaks into a growing focus on how research conducted by scholars from the humanities and social sciences can be integrated into natural science projects in order to create better solutions to societal challenges.

"This is an interdisciplinary collaboration that can benefit society as well as the arts and sciences. It is incredibly meaningful to be a part of these efforts, as we gain much more knowledge about the nature and possibilities of literature while doing research that can be of use in society," says Anne-Marie Mai.

The work has been developed under the guidance of Professor Rita Charon from Columbia University, who founded the discipline around 2000 on the basis of the idea that health professionals can improve their abilities to listen, analyze and engage with their patients by working methodologically with literature and arts. At the heart of narrative medicine is the term *narrative knowledge* and, increasingly even more used, *narrative competence*, which Charon defines as the ability "to understand the meaning and significance of stories through cognitive, symbolic, and affective means. This kind of knowledge provides a rich, resonant comprehension of a singular person's situation as it unfolds in time," as Charon writes in *Narrative medicine: A Model for Empathy, Reflection, Profession and Trust*.

"We have received an incredibly positive reception in the international field, and I consider Rita Charon our mentor – she is an extraordinary scholar who has been kind, generous, encouraging and thoughtful," says Mai. "She even fought her way through Manhattan in a snowstorm to reach me when we had our very first meeting. Charon's advice is always critical and constructive and her guidance has been of great value."

Mai introduced narrative medicine as a discipline at SDU after meeting a "very interesting gentleman" at the university's annual dinner party in 2013. His name was Kim Brixen; today, he is the Medical Director at Odense University Hospital, and at the time, he was Head of the Medical Institute. He, too, was interested in the potentials of literature and the medical humanities, and thus their collaboration began.

Despite the link between literature and medicine not being obvious to everyone, the researchers of narrative medicine at SDU are not afraid to speak of the multiple uses of literature, as they believe the potential is extensive. There are many purposes for the research project, but at the core of the research are the two questions: How can literature be useful in order to understand what it means to be healthy, sick, healing or dying? And how can a methodological systematic use of literature benefit peoples' physical and mental health, as well as their quality of life?

One approach is the teaching of medical students and health care professionals to increase particular skills, such as paying attention and listening closely to illness accounts. By training students' awareness of complex and ambiguous narratives, the power of language and metaphors, as well as the importance of imaginative skills, they will be equipped to improve their communicative competences and protect their sense of empathy in a health sector that is under immense pressure.

Another approach for narrative medicine is workshops (interventions) where patients or citizens meet in small groups with a

Rita Charon at a seminar, September 2019. Photo: Johan Thiesson

facilitator to read and discuss selected works of literature, which is called shared reading, often followed by creative writing exercises.

Maintaining humanity in medicine

Narrative knowledge or competence is an essential concept in the research conducted by the group at SDU, as these are seen as factors that can contribute to creating solutions to societal challenges such as unequal access to the health care system (health literacy) and decreasing empathy levels among doctors. Moreover, the scholars are convinced that it is possible to discuss the uses of literature without reducing it to merely an instrument. On the contrary, they believe that it can open the beauty, experiences and possibilities of literature to a wider range of people by making it available to different professions, as well as people from various socioeconomic backgrounds.

Anita Wohlmann, who joined Uses of Literature at SDU in 2017 as Assistant Professor and was promoted to Associate Professor in

2020, specializes in narrative medicine and American literature. From her perspective, narrative medicine is a clear example of the usefulness of literary studies in society at large, as the social benefits are easy to point out. Wohlmann highlights how doctors can benefit from being exposed to literature in particular.

"Health care professionals today face immense pressure to be efficient, and medical practice has become an increasingly difficult context to work in," Wohlmann explains. "Narrative medicine can act as an intervention into this culture – not to replace any aspects of the medical training – but to add a different perspective on what it means to be ill or to be a caregiver, as well as finding meaning in the interpersonal connection."

Through narrative medicine, medical professionals can stay curious and gain more tolerance for ambiguity and uncertainty. Its methods can make doctors' work lives richer by helping them maintain the humanity in their role, rather than ending up mechanically delivering medicine and diagnoses to one patient after the other. Even if there might not always be time to listen to the patients' full life stories, the awareness of the fact that each person has a complex story can improve the communication and treatment significantly.

Can literature make you a better doctor?

One specific part of the research program at SDU is a literary seminar for medical students, which is mandatory during the first year of their degree. This seminar was initially introduced by professor Anne-Marie Mai and professor Peter Simonsen in 2017.

Although it is a small seminar with just three hours of teaching for six weeks, it is significant in many ways. During the seminars, the medical students read literary fiction, conduct creative writing exercises, and discuss their interpretations of the texts. The texts vary and include writing by many contemporary Danish authors. The seminar was initially based on the anthology *Syg litteratur (Sick Literature)*, which is edited by the researchers Anne-Marie Mai and Peter Simonsen. Starting in the spring of 2022, the anthology is replaced by the anthology *Enhver sygdom er en fortælling* (*Every Illness is a Story*) edited by Anders Juhl Rasmussen, Cindie Aaen

Maagaard, Anette Bygum and Morten Sodemann. The new anthology represents the interdisciplinary collaboration between humanities and health through the selection of texts and its introduction to narrative medicine.

The seminar was established as part of a bigger trajectory called *People First*, where narrative medicine is one out of three seminars – the other two being health care psychology and health professional ethics. The three courses lead to an assignment where the students visit a chronically ill person in their home, and write about it afterwards.

In addition to the mandatory seminar for medical students at SDU for approximately 170 students each semester, Rasmussen and his team are also responsible for optional seminars that are offered for students of nursing, physio- and ergotherapy, pharmacy as well as midwives, all on their masters' level. The research group hopes to one day establish a second seminar in narrative medicine during the final years of a medical degree too. The students who had a seminar in narrative medicine during the first year of their bachelor degree will be able to return to the subject at the end of their master degree when they have attained more medical experience and are closer to beginning their professional careers. A stepping stone for such a seminar could be a summer school on narrative medicine for international and Danish medical and health care students.

Anders Juhl Rasmussen entered the field when the seminars of narrative medicine were established at SDU, and was appointed Associate Professor of Narrative medicine in 2019, which was the first professorship of Narrative medicine in Denmark. He has observed how the literature courses in the medical and health care programs have gradually gained more academic credibility, as well as increased acceptance among the students. When Rasmussen first began teaching, there was skepticism toward the seminar, especially from the medical students. However, its credibility has been strengthened by the fact that it is taught by both literary scholars and medical professionals in collaboration, and that the literary scholars engage in cross-disciplinary research with clinicians at SDU. Rasmussen is director of four of the courses, and he sees it as essential that teachers with different professional backgrounds are present at each seminar in order to ensure alignment and a clear connection between literature and medicine.

"The doctors who contribute to our teaching of narrative medicine can act as role models for the students in ways that we as literary scholars cannot. As a young doctor, you need role models, and therefore it is crucial that we can collaborate with these doctors who completely accept the methods of the humanities even though they cannot practice them," Rasmussen says.

The seminar and its methods are new and innovative, which means the researchers develop their approaches quickly, as they learn from the initial experiences and constantly adapt.

"The most important result of my work the last five years is the growing recognition that our seminar has gained at the medical school, because it is not guaranteed when you introduce a seminar that is so fundamentally different from the rest," says Rasmussen, adding that the students' evaluations are increasingly more positive, and the clinicians at the Odense University Hospital are now opening their minds to the approach.

An important aspect of the new discipline is that not everything can be learned from a PowerPoint slide or at the hospital. In order to become a good doctor, it is crucial to understand the importance of language, the choice of one word over another, and the use of metaphors and narratives. No one wants to confess their pain and fears to a robot, as humans we are willing to open up to other humans if they seem trustworthy and credible. Therefore, these abilities must be developed attentively. Rasmussen and his colleague Morten Sodemann call it a *style*. Besides learning medical skills, every new doctor must develop his or her own style; a way of being present in the room, and a way of speaking to the patients in order to make them feel comfortable enough to tell the doctor the *real* stories behind their symptoms.

The reflection and critical thinking required in taking part in the discussions around literature is exactly why the methods used in the humanities are effective. In that sense, the teaching differs significantly from the typical medical seminars, since nothing has to be memorized, and asking good questions is more important than having the right answers.

Anders Juhl Rasmussen and Nicklas Freisleben Lund at a Uses of Literature seminar in Svendborg, May 2019. Photo: David Binzer

"We present a seminar that is based on reflection and creativity, and we try to make art play a part in the education of these students," Rasmussen explains. "They will learn that a poem is metaphors and rhythm, but it is also something that offers an insight into the human condition in relation to illness, suffering, rehabilitation, care, nurture and much more."

Measuring empathy or impact

Associate Professor Rasmussen argues that the seminar in narrative medicine has the potential to strengthen the character and professionalism of the medical students. But can they *actually* become better doctors by reading, writing and discussing uses of language and narratives? Does the methodological systematic reading of literature and writing of their own stories lead to becoming a more empathetic clinician? Rasmussen would say yes, probably, but not automatically, as they are aware that the topic is debated among academics in the field. There are disagreements about whether it is even meaningful to measure empathy, and in that case, how to do so.

Empathy has become an important concept of the research in narrative medicine, as the lack of empathy among health care professionals is an issue that is often mentioned by patients and their relatives, and seems to be a growing societal challenge. A meta study made by Melanie Neumann et al. showed that medical students gradually lose empathy after entering the job market, which is something that is measured on the Jefferson Scale of Empathy, an instrument widely used to measure the self-perceived levels of empathy among health care workers. The scale consists of 20 questions and is used in the health care sector in more than 85 countries. Another study led by Justyn A. Charles et al. at SDU showed that the empathy levels among general practitioners decreased gradually during their working life, and that some had alarmingly low levels of empathy. There is growing agreement among scholars and health care professionals that this is a concerning tendency that must be dealt with.

Whether or not there is a causality – or only a correlation – between reading pieces of literary fiction and becoming more empathetic is a continuing discussion, and so far, there are no precise ways of measuring it. Rishi Goyal, a medical doctor affiliated with narrative medicine at Columbia University (who has visited SDU as a guest lecturer and taught students on the elective course at SDU) argues that by reading and discussing varying voices in literature, our sympathies for other people expand.

Rasmussen prefers to discuss *correlation* rather than *causality*, because it will, perhaps, never be possible to measure a direct and immediate causality. On the other hand, denying the potential of empathy improvement through aesthetic activities would take away a central argument for the necessity of the course as mandatory in medical education in his opinion.

Rasmussen asks questions that he deems urgent: "What can our research subjects gain from courses in narrative medicine from a clinical, health and scientific perspective? How can we document the impact of our research and interventions? That is what we need to reflect upon and write more about; which effects can we document?"

He explains that scholars from the natural and health sciences do not always recognize the concepts of knowledge that is used in the humanities, since the research is primarily both qualitative and conducted in smaller groups. Additionally, the patients and citizens participating in the groups may not always have the vocabulary to describe its effects. Practitioners who have experience with reading groups, for instance, are not afraid to say that it has positive effects, because they see the specific people who benefit from them. From a theoretical point of view, however, it is complicated to demonstrate the impact as "strong evidence".

The team at SDU continuously discusses whether such a correlation does exist, and how it can be investigated empirically and established theoretically, as the questions are almost philosophical in their nature. That is one of the challenges of working with health issues as a scholar of humanities: you are in between systems, theories and methods, which can make it difficult to get your research acknowledged within either field. Nonetheless, the researchers see great potential in expanding the interdisciplinary research between the humanities, social sciences and health science.

Complex stories from reality

Morten Sodemann, who is a medical doctor and professor of global and migrant health at SDU, is one of the teachers at the seminar in narrative medicine. With decades of experience in the medical field, he speaks confidently on the basis of his countless experiences as a doctor.

"For many years I have been saddened to see what happens to young doctors and nurses, how quickly they become cynical, harsh and lose their sense of empathy after entering their professional lives. Either they learn to adjust to this attitude of harshness, or they burn out. Many forget the human aspect of their role – the care and human understanding – because of the idea that better communication with patients would demand more of their precious time, and would only make their jobs more difficult," says Sodemann.

He argues that there is a strong false narrative among health care professionals about the lack of time for longer conversations with patients, and this point of view is quickly adopted by young doctors who enter the field. Sodemann believes that it is a grave misunderstanding. In fact, he says, the health care system could save time and resources if they dedicated 45 minutes for a longer interview with the patient at the beginning of each treatment, and focused on listening attentively and asking open and critical questions. In the long run, it would actually *save time*, because they would avoid misdiagnosing or overlooking important symptoms, thereby potentially giving the patient the wrong treatment.

"Our hope is that the lessons in narrative medicine will protect against burnout in such a way that the patients will meet doctors who are less cynical and more empathetic, who take the time to listen, and who understand the person in front of them and their specific symptoms," he says. "Doctors who can translate statistics and experience into a meaningful understanding of a specific person's life and create a tailor-made treatment for that person."

Sodemann often tells the story of a patient who once came to him after years of pain and unsuccessful treatments. He was an elderly man with a refugee background who had seen the doctor several times because of trouble with his knee, and eventually he had lost his job as a bus driver because of the pain. After spending some time talking with the man and listening attentively to his story, Sodemann discovered that the man was a survivor of torture that had caused him to loose control over vital body functions, which meant that he had to wear a diaper while working as a bus driver. The man had become so obsessed with the fear that the passengers could tell he was wearing it, that he started calling in sick and feeling worse; the images of the torture began coming back to him and he became increasingly confused and disoriented, which in the end led him to lose his job. He *did* feel pain in his body, but the essence of his problem was not pain, but trauma. Sodemann never would have discovered this underlying issue, had he not paid attention and asked curious, critical questions about the man's story, and these abilities are exactly what the professor wants to teach medical students through narrative medicine.

"If patients continuously experience a lack of understanding, they will begin to withdraw in order to avoid exposing themselves too much, but they will still seek recognition and give small cues about what is really going on," explains Sodemann. "In order to intercept them, you need a literary sensibility that medical school will not normally teach you. Narrative medicine can sharpen your senses in order for you to understand what the stories are really about."

Shared reading and creating writing workshops for ill or vulnerable citizens

In addition to the teaching of narrative medicine for health care professionals, the group of scholars has conducted research on the effects of shared reading and creative writing workshops among people who are vulnerable or recovering from illness, in order to investigate how the methods of narrative medicine can be applied directly to patients or citizens. So far, workshops have been held for survivors of cancer, people suffering from alcohol abuse, people with arthritis and sclerosis, and for elderly men who have recently left the job market.

Professor (WSO) Anette Søgaard Nielsen, is the leader of the Unit for Clinic Alcohol Research (UCAR) at SDU, and has worked with narrative medicine since she established the first shared reading and creative writing workshops for former alcohol abusers in cooperation with Anne-Marie Mai in 2016.

Mai particularly remembers one of their first workshops at an alcohol clinic in Odense, where she had invited the two writers Trisse Gejl and Julie Sten-Knudsen to facilitate the groups. The participants were very skeptical at first, but were intrigued by the professionalism of the two writers, as well as the free coffee and cake. However, the effect was rather powerful in the end. Mai recalls one person who was very scarred by his alcohol abuse and thought he had lost his memory. While participating in the writing exercise, the participants had to repeat the line "I remember…" and fill in their own memories. Suddenly, the man recalled the memory of sitting in a greenhouse as a little boy, smelling the scent of a tomato plant and listening to raindrops hitting the glass ceiling.

Anne-Marie Mai (left), in conversation with Anne-Marie Søndergaard Christensen and Rita Felski at a Uses of Literature seminar in Svendborg, May 2019. Photo: David Binzer

"In a glimpse he remembered that he had not always been an alcoholic, but once been a little boy with a body full of senses and an openness towards the world," says Mai.

Since then, Anette Søgaard Nielsen has conducted research on similar workshops for several different patient groups. Because this sort of treatment is still new, the researchers are conducting qualitative studies among the participants to gain a better picture of how the workshops affect them, but it is Søgaard Nielsen's clear impression that reading and writing can increase the patients' abilities to reflect and understand themselves and the world around them.

"The workshops can be considered a strategy in the rehabilitation of patients who have been very ill – a form of rehabilitation in living again, of being in the world, and being able to comprehend and process it," Søgaard Nielsen says. "It seems to have the effect that the participants get a heightened sense of their own abilities, a more nuanced view of the world and a broadened perspective."

Søgaard Nielsen sees a lot of potential in developing the methods of the shared reading and creative writing workshops. While they currently work with smaller groups – where individuals are subject to qualitative interviews or surveys in order to measure a possible effect – the scholars might be able to expand their research design in the future by using more standardized tools, such as larger control groups, randomized selection of participants, and even scans of brain activity or studies of biological markers.

Fighting stigma with DECIDE

As part of the new research project *DECIDE* – led by Associate Professor and medical doctor Maja Thiele at the Centre for Liver Research – Anders Juhl Rasmussen is facilitating reading and writing workshops for people with health issues associated with liver damage, in order to counter the stigma they often face in the health care system. This group often experiences being stigmatized as "alcoholics" or "obese" and because of these attitudes from health care professionals, they tend to hesitate to seek help from a doctor.

The design of *DECIDE* is that a small group of five or six people meet eight times over the course of two months and read a piece of literary fiction by writers such as Karen Blixen, Peter Seeberg or Tove Ditlevsen. They spend the first hour listening to a chosen text read aloud by the facilitator, and then they make a close reading of the text. During the second hour, the participants write a story of their own and read it aloud for the group and receive feedback from the facilitator.

When reading the poem *Lola* by Tove Ditlevsen, some of the participants might ask questions such as: Is the tragic protagonist completely on her own? Who is the person who suddenly recognizes her? They might ask thematic questions about loneliness, community, and about going too far down the wrong roads in life.

"Some of the participants have completed only the most basic levels of education and do not have any preconditions to reading such type of literary work, but besides improving their ability to use language – what we call their 'health literacy' – they sit there with a group of strangers and suddenly experience that the text has something to offer on a deep personal level. It makes them ask new questions that can be of importance in their own lives," says Rasmussen. "There are feelings, sensations and behavioral patterns we all share, that become apparent when reading good literary texts."

In *DECIDE*, the researchers work particularly with stigma as a theme, and besides investigating whether participation in a workshop can help the citizens themselves by strengthening their self-esteem and opening their world to new perspectives, the researchers also want to fight stigma in the health care system concerning the issues they face.

In addition to writing academic articles on the background of the project, the team is working on creating innovative and experimental outcomes of the workshops. At the end of the process, they will select texts from the creative writing exercises and ask their authors to read them aloud in a sound studio. Professional illustrators will then create animations to follow the sound bites, and the finished works will be displayed on a website that will be promoted nationwide in Denmark and among health care professionals in particular. The idea is that the authenticity of the participants' voices will make the stories relatable without exposing them personally.

The researchers hope that the project will have a significant impact on especially health professionals who often have strong prejudice against people with risk factors for developing liver disease, alcoholism and diabetes/obesity, perhaps because medical professionals are often "health-conscious individuals with a high sense of self-discipline," Rasmussen argues.

He believes that the media production can have a real impact, despite it not being what researchers typically do in the field. The project is inspired by the British campaign *What's Up With Everyone,* which was made on the initiative of Paul Crawford, a professor of health humanities at The University of Nottingham. The website, which features voices and animations, and has been seen by five million young Brits, addresses issues such as perfectionism and loneliness – feelings common among young people – as it aims to increase mental health literacy among youth. The campaign made by the researchers from SDU will have a different style, as the target group is different, but the fundamental ideas and ambitions are the same.

DECIDE is a project supported by funding from the Novo Nordisk Foundation, yet it builds on the experiences gained during the Uses of Literature project, and Rasmussen underlines that his work on the new project would not have existed without the knowledge and methods developed over the past five years.

Read like a man

Another reading workshop is the project *Læs som en mand (Read Like a Man)*, which has been established by Peter Simonsen, Professor of European Literature at the Department for the Study of Culture at SDU and part of the founding group behind Uses of Literature.

Read Like a Man was initiated in cooperation with Associate Professor and manager of Human Health, Anna Paldam Folker, as an integrated part of Uses of Literature, and has focused on working with healthy elderly men in the ages 65-75 who face retirement – a major life transition that can be a sensitive period in life.

The project is aimed at this particular group of men, since studies have shown that there is a significant risk of decreasing quality of life for men in this period of their lives, as they leave the job market, which has provided identity as well as structure and substance of daily life. On that basis, a team of researchers from SDU has developed the project, where they invited a small group of men in this transitional phase to join a reading workshop.

Responsible for the literary component of *Read Like a Man,* Simonsen is interested in discovering how literature can be used to understand and promote health in a broad sense. He is interested in looking at factors beyond diet, alcohol consumption, and exercise habits; rather, he seeks to explore how literature and art can influence our health and quality of life. The hypothesis is that reading literary fiction in a communal setting can contribute to a heightened sense of meaning and quality of life, and in the end, lead to strengthened health.

"Participants say that the workshop has helped them understand themselves and their families better," says Simonsen. "They find pleasure in participating in the reading group, and are surprised by their own ability to discuss poems and have positive experiences related to literature."

Inspired by the practice developed by the British organization *The Reader* and the Danish organization *Læseforeningen*, Simonsen has taken a course to become a certified reading guide at the latter, which means that he follows their methodology of reading two selected texts – one prose and one poem – aloud, and having a joint discussion afterwards. Simonsen only selects literature of high quality, which he defines as texts encompassing linguistic precision and nuance, complexity and depth in thought and emotion, human gravity in theme, as well as a capacity to inspire new thinking and feeling in the reader.

By leading reading groups for several weeks, Simonsen has observed safe spaces being created where the participants can discuss sensitive topics such as sexuality and bodily decay in a respectful and humoristic atmosphere. For many, the reading group has become a place where it is acceptable to share their vulnerabilities and where thoughts are met with recognition, according to Simonsen.

"We are interested in how literature is used – and particularly how aging men can use it during an important life transition – which is an entirely new area of research. It is also a rare project that combines literary studies with health science and attempts to conduct empirical research."

The research team is now analyzing the data in order to present their conclusions based on qualitative interviews. Due to its interdisciplinary nature, the project called for interdisciplinary cooperation, which is why Simonsen has worked closely together with the philosopher Anna Paldam Folker, who contributed with perspectives on what it means to live a "meaningful life" and with anthropologist and PhD-student Mette Marie Kristensen, who has conducted systematic interviews and analyzed the data.

As a literary scholar, Simonsen is able to select high-quality literature that the participants in the group might relate to, be shocked by, or that might move them in ways that change their ways of thinking and open their minds to new ideas and conversations. He was curious about what kinds of texts participants might like and found that it was impossible to predict – some liked texts about elderly males that made for easy identification, some preferred being introduced to new and alien characters, moods, times and places. Conversely, some liked and were intrigued by complicated formal structures often hard to reduce to a clear meaning, while others seemed to prefer a more easily understandable realistic prose style. The most important thing, he has gathered, is the reading guide's enthusiasm and ability to make the text's aesthetic qualities felt and shared, to make participants aware of the linguistic precision, and to encourage exploration of complexity of thought and emotion. On a good day – which is not every day, Simonsen jokes – the guide will make participants feel inspired to see their lives in new, more meaningful and more connected ways.

This type of interdisciplinary work and the use of empirical methods within the literary field that *Read Like a Man* has fostered are new approaches for Simonsen, and he hopes to continue with this type of work at the permanent research center for Uses of Literature that SDU has established.

In addition, the research group hopes to create a handbook that can document the effects of the literary workshops for retired men, and thus reach a larger audience in order to tell about the potentials and uses of literature in a broader sense.

Dementia and Creativity

Aging populations bring along new challenges, as our societies' oldest people live longer lives and experience illnesses and different types of dementia that are common in old age. Scholars from Uses of Literature have looked at several aspects of the topics in contemporary literature to understand the representations and how literature can be a source of comfort and knowledge for the elderly, people with dementia and their relatives.

In the project *DEMENS ID* (*Dementia ID*) – an interdisciplinary collaboration between the Faculty of Health at SDU, Rudersdal Municipality, the Danish Association for Alzheimers (*Alzeimerforeningen*)*,* and scholars from the humanities – citizens are closely involved in understanding dementia and the uncertainties around it.

"We use literary texts and workshop-facilitated guided reading to work with dementia patients and their relatives and caregivers to see if this improves their understanding of ethical dilemmas in dementia care, promote their self-efficacy, and thereby improve their management of ethical dilemmas," Simonsen explains.

Postdoc Marie-Elisabeth Lei Holm is mainly responsible for developing and testing a corpus of texts for use in this project. Holm has designed workshops and chosen literary material that can foster dialogue around ethical dilemmas in dementia care.

In order to exchange ideas and further develop the newest theories on the subject, Simonsen organized two symposia on Creativity and Dementia in 2018 and 2019 in cooperation with Professor Gitte Rasmussen from the Department of Language and Communication at SDU. They brought together leading scholars from different disciplines from both Europe and the US.

Dementia and Interpretive Risk

Alastair Morrison has been part of the Uses of Literature project as an Assistant Professor, and has focused on narrative representations of dementia in his research. His main project explores relationships between literary representations of dementia, and the practical realities of care for people with dementia.

In his research, Morrison argues that "self-conscious literary representation can help us conceptualize, accept, and prepare for this circumstance of interpretive risk in care." In the literature he studied, Morrison found a pattern in the texts dealing with dementia – in their ways of reflecting on what it means to represent and speak on behalf of people who have these illnesses. This pattern extends across different styles of writing: in poetry, this means explorations of the limits of the lyric form and how much the poetic speaker can say about people outside of the poem. In novels, it often means narrators who speak uncertainly on behalf of other characters, in what Morrison refers to as "narrative surrogacy".

The risk of speaking on behalf of people with dementia is a very real one, a challenge experienced by health care professionals as well as relatives of people suffering from the illness. These issues are mirrored in literature describing dementia, which draws attention to the difficulty and uncertainty around speaking for people who aren't able to communicate for themselves – and the necessary risk of interpreting their needs.

Alastair Morrison and Rita Felski at a Uses of Literature seminar in Nyborg, May 2017. Photo: David Binzer

"In both clinical and family settings, it is sometimes necessary for caregivers to make decisions that normally ought to be made by the person themselves, sometimes in situations where that person cannot be adequately consulted," explains Morrison. "This is an unsatisfactory circumstance that brings with it an inevitable risk of error, inappropriate action, and even harm. And yet to refuse these decisions would sometimes be a greater harm."

Morrison elaborates on his ideas in the forthcoming book chapter *Other Voices: George Oppen, Dementia, and the Echo of Lyric*, which will be part of the book, *A Poetic Language of Aging*, edited by Oddgeir Synnes and Olga Lehmann, and published by Bloomsbury.

A life changing turn

When Morrison began working on his project on how contemporary literature approaches and shapes responses to dementia, his approach to research and teaching was of a traditional literary kind. While conducting the research, however, he became increasingly committed to topics of illness and health care, as he began collaborating with leaders in the field of narrative medicine, going to conferences where he met doctors and health researchers. Eventually, Morrison decided to change his career path rather drastically and pursue a degree in medicine, which meant that he enrolled in the medical school of McMaster University in his home country Canada in 2020. By combining his knowledge from the humanities with medical training, he hopes to incorporate the humanistic research and teaching methods into medical practice and contribute to solving new kinds of tasks and problems in contemporary society.

"Medicine became more and more fascinating to me as I learned more about it, to the point where giving papers about illness without helping sick people did not feel like enough anymore," Morrison explains.

In the article *Beyond bad faith: Cultural criticism and instrumentality,* which was published in the renowned journal *Criticism* in 2019, Morrison explores "theoretical considerations related to "using" literature, or thinking about the social consequences of different texts and styles of reading." The article seeks to explain why the discipline of English literary studies "has often rejected goal-oriented applications of literary studies: there is the position that literary study is very important, but there is also a strong aversion to even guessing about what it might actually do for anyone, as though we would be undermining the subject by instrumentalizing it".

Morrison wanted to explain how these ideas arose, a story which is closely connected to the secularization of Britain, in order to make space for possible change. He argues, that the attitude can be avoided and that research in the humanities can be done differently.

"A humanistic education enriches students in ways that are hard to predict or quantify. But the same is true of other forms of education too, and we do not hesitate to talk about how scientific knowledge, or mathematical knowledge, or political knowledge will be relevant for attaining specific societal goals," Morrison argues.

"In the article I did not talk much about medicine. But as I met more doctors and health scholars, I came to believe very strongly that a humanistic education is a major – and very practical! – asset for a health care provider in many situations. If the article is about how literary studies can serve instrumental goals, my entry into medicine is an attempt to make it do that."

Last Years of Life

In the research project *Last Years of Life* Peter Simonsen and postdoc Nicklas Freisleben Lund analyze representations of the last years of life of fictional characters. Their research is a part of The Danish Aging Research Center's (DARC) interdisciplinary project with the overarching theme *The last years of life – health, treatment and well-being*. The project, which is funded by the Velux Foundation, comprises research areas such as Public Health Science, General Practice, and the Humanities.

Lund and Simonsen's research focuses on the contemporary Scandinavian and Anglophone "gerontological literature", which refers to literature about aging, old age and the end of life. The aim is to produce knowledge about the meaning of aging and the last years of life by informing us about what it might feel like and what cultural implications it may have that we live longer and longer lives in relatively good health, but that these lives are 'finite'. As an additional outcome, the researchers plan to communicate the findings to doctors in order to "improve their ability to understand and communicate with their many very old patients," Simonsen says.

The output so far – the project concludes in 2023 – among other things includes the chapter *Happy Ends? Aldring, trivsel og senlivskvalitet i ældrelitterature* in the forthcoming cross-disciplinary anthology *Det gode ældreliv*.

Furthermore, Simonsen and Lund have pursued a quite original angle on literary gerontology, which is poetry about aging, a genre that has largely been overlooked in the field so far. In their forthcoming article *Old songs from the welfare state, Nordic gerontological poetry and lyric gerontology,* Simonsen and Lund write that "poetry differs from, does something else and is experienced differently than narrative prose." As a genre, poetry has affordances that differ from those of narrative prose, as it can "capture ambivalences, mixed emotions, hopes and fears relating to aging," they write.

According to Lund, the genre can expand our understanding of life in old age and depict it in all of its diversity, which makes it an interesting subject of study.

"Poetry has the ability to present other perspectives on the experiences of aging. While narrative prose often seeks to create life stories with clear developments and connections, poetry has the potential to represent experiences that are fragmented, complex and provide multitudes of little glimpses that can give an impression of the diversity of life in old age," says Lund. "In a single collection of poetry, you can find poems about dying friends, the fun of having casual sex, the frustrations of using a walker, and the joys of having grandchildren."

In general, literature dealing with old age can offer a space for reflections about the complexities of a life phase that more and more people are experiencing due to aging populations and demographic changes. Reading and discussing literature on the topic can enhance our understanding of and expectations towards this phase – whether we are already old or on our way there – and it can contribute to the discussions about meaningfulness in the last years of life.

In addition to *Last Years of Life*, Simonsen also leads the project *Reading Retirement*, where the group analyzes and characterizes contemporary novels about life in retirement. They explore the concept of "creative aging" through studies of reading groups and the use of audiobooks as two different forms of reading habits; one that is communal, the other solitary.

The life knowledge in illness metaphors

While some parts of the research in narrative medicine is experimental and highly innovative, the classic methods of the humanities and literary studies are still essential in the work they do at SDU.

One example is a new book by Associate Professor Anita Wohlmann (to be published in 2022) in which she looks at illness metaphors in contemporary illness narratives.

A central metaphor is the one which compares illness to a fight; for instance, the notion that someone "fights against cancer" is a widespread and frequently used metaphor that is highly criticized.

With a background in American literature, Wohlmann analyzed the use of this particular metaphor in selected works by Audre Lorde, Susan Sontag, David Foster Wallace, Arthur Frank and Siri Hustvedt.

The metaphor of fighting a serious illness has many disadvantages and can stigmatize people who are not able to recover from their illness. It can be seen as limiting, and there is a component of the expression related to a Darwinian worldview in which only the fittest survive. In addition, the metaphor can be tied to American individualism, the importance of self-reliance, and independence from the government. The underlying idea is that if you are strong enough, you will make it on your own. However, Wohlmann adds, every metaphor is false: Illness is not a battle, it is something that happens to our bodies that we have to deal with.

Despite the metaphor's many problems, Wohlmann found – to her surprise – that the selected writers do not criticize or reject the metaphor, but rather embrace and reinvent it in order to create new meanings or empowerment.

"I was astonished to find that instead of rejecting the metaphor and looking for new ones, these writers continued to use it. In this sense, my research was greatly influenced by my participation in the Uses of Literature project, because I realized that we can look at these uses of metaphors in a more positive way," Wohlmann says.

"In addition to being suspicious and criticizing it, we can explore what we can learn from these writers in how they deal with a metaphor that is problematic. I find it very interesting how they approach the metaphor, and in this sense my research was very much inspired by Rita Felski's work. Her research has encouraged me to take seriously and conceptualize the strategies of reuse and creative misuse, which the writers I examine are employing when they tackle the battle metaphor."

For example, in *The Cancer Journals*, Audre Lorde broadens the meaning of the battle metaphor and takes ownership of it. Lorde connects the metaphor of fighting with something she has done her entire life as an activist against racism and homophobia.

"Lorde broadens this idea of fighting and says: there are female fighters too; there are Amazons, and like me, they have lost a breast

*Anita Wohlmann at a seminar with Rita Charon and Rita Felski, September 2019
Photo by: Johan Thiesson*

in order to become better fighters. Lorde established a relation to the Amazons through this metaphor, and this strategy affords a new, liberating and empowering significance to this worn-out metaphor," Wohlmann says.

Working on illness narratives has inspired Wohlmann to look into metaphors related to old age and aging, as there are several interesting and problematic metaphors related to this life phase. The use of metaphors, more generally, can be of relevance for a broader range of people, as there is a "life knowledge" in the varied usability of metaphors that close readings and literary analysis can bring to the surface, Wohlmann argues.

Creating new networks for narrative medicine
Narrative medicine is still a relatively new discipline at SDU, but the research area has undergone immense development and gained growing recognition in Denmark, as well as internationally. Several scholars from different disciplines at SDU have been highly engaged in topics related to Medical Humanities during the recent

years and the group from Uses of Literature have actively sought contact and cooperation with leading international scholars within the field.

In 2017, the researchers from Uses of Literature organized a three-day event on Narrative medicine in cooperation with The Nordic Network for Narratives in Medicine. The event featured workshops and discussions between prominent scholars such as Professor Rita Charon from Columbia University, Niels Bohr Professor Rita Felski, and writer and Professor Emeritus David B. Morris from University of Virginia.

In 2018 Professor Emeritus Arthur Frank from University of Calgary visited SDU to give a lecture on *Vulnerable Reading: The Company of Shakespeare,* in which he elaborated on his theories on the practice of vulnerable reading as a form of companionship in times of illness, disability and sorrow.

Anita Wohlmann and her colleagues at SDU have been particularly interested in the outreach of their research on Narrative medicine. Among other things, Wohlmann has established a network for German-speaking scholars working with narrative medicine in order to create visibility and gather the experts in the field to foster cooperation and new connections across Germany, Austria, Switzerland and Denmark. The network organizes workshops and distributes information through a mailing list, which Wohlmann coordinates.

In December 2019, Wohlmann organized an interdisciplinary workshop in Medical Humanities in collaboration with Professor Susanne Michl at Charité University Medical Center Berlin. The workshop *Data and Stories in Digital Healthcare,* which was funded by the Volkswagen Stiftung grant for *Mixed Methods for Medical Humanities,* examined the connections between the humanities, medicine and data science. It focused on "the variety of forms in which information about health and illness travels between different stakeholders, such as patients and health care professionals."

As a result of her work in the past five years, in addition to writing several academic articles and book chapters, Wohlmann has written a German handbook on narrative medicine, which she has co-edited with colleagues from the Technical University Munich.

Rita Felski on the left and Rita Charon on the right at a seminar, September 2019. Photo by: Johan Thiesson

The handbook is a compilation of ten articles about the use of literary texts, pedagogies and discussions with medical students, the aim is mainly to address the instructors who teach medical students and are inspired by literary studies and interested in trying new approaches. The network for narrative medicine has received several requests from instructors, doctors and teachers in the medical field who are interested in applying the methods of narrative medicine, and the practical handbook is written to address this interest and the uncertainties that might occur, as well as offer concrete advice, inspiration and exercises.

In addition, Wohlmann has been appointed co-editor of *Age, Culture, Humanities*, which is an open-access journal that will be supported by SDU and the Royal Danish Library in the future. With this role, she hopes to establish the field even more firmly in the years to come.

Researchers who have been part of the work package on Narrative medicine during the Uses of literature project:

Alastair Morrison
Anders Juhl Rasmussen
Anette Søgaard Nielsen
Anita Wohlmann
Anna Paldam Folker
Anne-Marie Mai
Anne-Marie Søndergaard Christensen
Cindie Aaen Maagaard
Emily Hogg
Helene Snede Andersen
Helle Ploug Hansen
Josefine Ranfeldt Andersen
Marie-Elisabeth Lei Holm
Merethe Kirstine Kousgaard Andersen
Mette Marie Kristensen
Morten Sodemann
Peter Simonsen
Sara Seerup Laursen
Tine Riis Andersen

The Ten Most Important Publications from 2016-2021
In alphabetical order:

2016

Felski, R. (2016): "Comparison and Translation: A Perspective from Actor-network-theory", *Comparative Literary Studies*, 53, 4, Penn State University Press.

Felski, R. (2016): "Introduction", *New Literary History*, 47, 2-3 special issue: "Recomposing the Humanities with Bruno Latour", Johns Hopkins University Press.

Felski, R. (2016): "Attachment", *Textual Practice*, 30, 7, Routledge.

Felski, R. (2016): "Entanglement and Animosity: Literature and Religion", *Religion and Literature,* 48, 2 (2017), University of Notre Dame.

Haarder, J.H. (2016): "A Story We Are Part of. Introducing Performative Biographism by way of reading Karl Ove Knausgård's My Struggle (and vice versa)", in H. Skov Nielsen (ed.), *Expectations*, Medusa.

Kettunen, P., Lundberg, U., Österberg, M. and Petersen, K. (2016): "The Nordic model and the rise and fall of Nordic cooperation", in Johan Strang (ed.), *Nordic Cooperation: A European region in transition*, (Routledge series on global order studies, Vol. 8), Routledge.

Mai, A.-M. (2016): *Danish Literature of the 20th and early 21st Century*, 1. ed., (University of Southern Denmark Studies in Danish Languages and Literatures vol. 131), University Press of Southern Denmark.

Mai, A.-M. (2016): *Galleri 66: En historie om nyere dansk litteratur*, 1. ed., Gyldendal.

Marx, P. and Nguyen, C. (2016): "Are the unemployed less politically involved?" a comparative study of internal political efficacy, *European Sociological Review*, 32, 5, Oxford University Press.

Schramm, M. and Ring Petersen, A. (2016): "Postmigration. Mod et nyt kritisk perspektiv på migration og kultur", *K & K*, årg. 44, nr. 22.

2017

Felski. R. and Anker E.S (eds.) (2017). *Critique and Postcritique*, Duke University Press.

Felski, R. (2017). "Postcritical Reading". *American Book Review*, 38(5). This special issue of ABR is devoted to responses to Felskis recent research.

Hogg, E. J. (2020). "Human Rights, the Family and the Bildungsroman in Goretti Kyomuhendo's Waiting: A Novel of Uganda at War". *Textual Practice*.

Mai, A-M. (2017). "Breaking new ground: Danish Poets in the Intersection between Modernism and Postmodernism". In D. Ringgaard, & M. Rosendahl Thomsen (eds.), *Danish literature as World Literature* (1 ed., Vol. 1). [9] Bloomsbury Academic.

Mai, A-M. (2017). "Poets in New York". In D. Ringgaard (ed.), *Nordic Literature: A comparative history*. Volume I: Spatial Nodes (1 ed.). John Benjamins Publishing Company.

Petersen, K., & Béland, D. (2017). "Exploring social policy ideas and language". In P. Kennett, & N. Lendvai-Bainton (eds.), *Handbook of European Social Policy*. Edward Elgar Publishing, Incorporated.

Rasmussen, A. J. (2017). "What does it mean to listen, and how can it be learned?". *BMJ Medical Humanities*.

Simonsen, P. (2017). "'Forstod hun hvor frustrerede og ulykkelige de var?': Demanding Happiness in Nikolaj Zeuthen's 'Verdensmestre': En historie fra oo'erne". *Scandinavian Studies*.

Schramm, M., Albrecht, A., & Venzl, T. (eds.) (2017). *Literatur und Anerkennung: Wechselwirkungen und Perspektiven*. LIT Verlag. FOLIES.

Yazell, B. (2017). "Steinbeck's Migrants: Families on the Move and the Politics of Resource Management". *Modern Fiction Studies*, 63(3).

2018

Christensen, A-M. S. (2018). "'Life and World Are One'. World, Self and Ethics in the Work of Levinas and Wittgenstein". In O. Kuusela, M. Ometita, & Tucan (Eds.), *Wittgenstein and Phenomenology*. Routledge Research in Phenomenology.

Felski, R. (2018). "Identification and Critique". In F. Kelleter, & A. Starre (Eds.), *Projecting American Studies: Essays on Theory, Methos and Practice*. Universitätsverlag Winter (PR)

Fessenbecker, P. (2018). "The Gospel of Work". In *Oxford Bibliographies in Victorian Literature*. Oxford University Press.

Haarder, J. H., Simonsen, P., & Schwartz, C. (2018). "Hvem kan tale for prekariatet – og hvorfor? In the Ghetto med Kristian Bang Foss, Morten Pape, Yahya Hassan, Karina Pedersen og prinsesserne fra blokken". *Edda*, 105(3), 185-202.

Hogg, E. (2018). "Human Rights, the Family and the Bildungsroman in Goretti Kyomuhendo's waiting: A Novel of Uganda at War. *Textual Practice*. (e-pub ahead of print – Aug 13, 2018).

Mai, A-M. (2018). *Digteren Dylan*. Gyldendal (PR)

Wohlmann, A. (2018). "Naturalist Sentimentalism: Ageing Between Hopefulness and Decline in Rebecca Harding Davis's Short Fiction". *European Journal of English Studies*, 22(1).

Yazell, B. (2018). "Irish-Israelism: Recognition the Politics of race and belonging in 'Cyclops'". *James Joyce Quarterly*, 53(3-4).

Yazell, B. (2018). "The Politics of Precarity in William Gibson's 'Bridge' Trilogy. *Studies in the Fantastic*, 6, 39-69.

Aarhus, M. G. (2018). "Skammen og dens brødre: Arbejdsløshed, maskulinitet og klassekamp". *K & K*, 46(125), 179-198.

2019

Anderson, A., Felski, R. & Moi, T. (2019): *Character. Three Inquiries in Literary Studies*, The University of Chicago Press.

Hogg, E. (2019): "Displacement", in T*he Routledge Companion to Twenty-First Century Literary Fiction* (eds. Robert Eaglestone & Daniel O'Gorman), Routledge.

Hsuan, H. & Yazell; B. (2019): "Post-Apocalyptic Geographies and Structural Appropriation", in *Routledge Companion to Transnational American Studies*, Routledge.

Mai, A.-M. (ed.) (2019): *Litteratur i brug*, Spring.

Maurer, K. & Schramm, M. (2019): "Between Nation-State and Transnational Openings", in *The German Quarterly* 92(4)

Morrison, A. (2019): "Beyond bad faith", in *Criticism: a quarterly for literature and the arts* 61(2)

Ploug Hansen, H., Seerup Laursen, S., Zwisler, A.D. & Juhl Rasmussen, A. (2019): "'I'm sure that there is something healing in the writing process'", in *Tidsskrift for Forskning i Sygdom og Samfund* 16(31)

Schwartz, C. & Mai, A.-M. (2019): "Vægt og vilje. Om menneskebilleder i Sundhedsstyrelsens vægttabsguide", in Menneskebilleder (eds. Finn Collin, David Budtz Pedersen & Frederik Stjernfeldt), Hans Reitzels Forlag.

Simonsen, P. (2019): "Poetry and age", in *Encyclopedia of Gerontology and Population Aging* (eds. Danan Gu & Matthew E. Dupre), Springer.

Wohlmann, A. (ed.): *Disability Writing*, De Gruyter.

2020

Chynoweth, A., Lynch, B., Petersen, K. & Smed, S. (eds.) (2020). *Museums and Social Change*. Routledge

Felski, R. (2020). *Hooked: Art and Attachment*. Chicago University Press.

Felski, R. & Muecke, S. (2020). *Latour and the Humanities*. Johns Hopkins University Press.

Felski, R. (2020). "Good Vibrations", *American Literary History*, 32, 2. Oxford University Press.

Hogg, E. & Simonsen, P. (2020). "The potential of precarity? Imagining vulnerable connection in Chris Dunkley's The Precariat and Amy Liptrot's The Outrun, *Criticism: a quarterly for literature and the arts*, 62, 1. Wayne State University.

Mai, A.M. (ed.) (2020). *New Approaches to Bob Dylan*. University Press of Southern Denmark.

Simonsen, P. & Haarder, J.H. (eds.) with Dr C. Claire Thompson (University College London) as journal editor (2020). Theme issue: "Precarity in Scandinavian Literature", *Scandinavica*, vol. 59, issue 2. Department of Scandinavian Studies, University College London Gower Street.

Rasmussen, A.J. & Sodemann, M. (2020). "Narrativ medicin som nyt, interdisciplinært felt", *Ugeskrift for Laeger*, 182, 29.

Wohlmann, A., & Michl, S. (2020). "The gains of reduction in translational processes: illness blogs and clinical cases", *Humanities and social sciences communications*, 6. Palgrave Communications

Yazell, B. (2020). "A Sociology of Failure: Migration and Narrative Method in US Climate Fiction", *Configurations*, 28, 2. Johns Hopkins University Press.

2021

Freisleben Lund, N. et al. (2021). "Pandemiens muse – Om den danske coronadigtning 2020-2021", SPRING – *tidsskrift for moderne litteratur* 49.

Hogg, E. and Simonsen, P. (2021). *Precarity in Contemporary Literature and Culture*, Bloomsbury Academic.

Lei Holm, M-E. (2021) "Are we Still Ourselves?". *Intima. Journal of Narrative Medicine*. 22. January 2

Mai, A-M. (2021). *Danish Literature from 1000 til 1900*. University Press of Southern Denmark.

Rasmussen, A.J. et al. ed. (2021). *Narrativ medicin i undervisning og praksis*. Gads forlag.

Schwartz, C. (2021). *Take me to neverland*, Forlaget Spring

Schwartz, C. & Felski, R. (2021). "Gender, Love and Recognition in I Love Dick and The Other Woman", *European Journal of Women's Studies*.

Wohlmann, A. (2021). "Green Medicine: Ecofeminist Readings of Women's Medication Narratives", in *Controlling Bodies, Constructing Minds (Post-)Feminist Identity Politics in the Biomedical Age* (eds. Johanna Heil, Anna Thiemann), Peter Lang.

Aarhus, M.G. and Haarder, J.H. (2021)."The Unemployed", in *Citizen Categories in the Danish Welfare State*, (eds. Køber, J.V., Olsen, N., Jønsson, H.V).University Press of Southern Denmark.

Aarhus, M.G. and Simonsen, P. (2021). "Theater of the Precariat: Staging Precarity in Alexander Zeldin's Love", *Contemporary Literature*, Vol. 61, Number 3.